"A compelling and freeing book that addresses one of the issues of our day: dealing with the effects of sex before marriage. This book will not only help those who've failed, but hopefully it will be used by God to help many to stand firm."

—Dennis Rainey
Executive Director of FamilyLife
(a division of Campus Crusade for Christ)

"We live in a world that often chooses not to acknowledge the very real physical, spiritual, and emotional consequences of premarital sex. *Reclaiming Intimacy* is an indispensable resource for counselors, for friends of those who have made bad choices, and for any person who has ever been caught in the trap of counterfeit intimacy. I wholeheartedly recommend this book."

—Dr. Greg Smalley
President of Today's Family

"Heather Jamison opens a door that has been closed and forgotten for a long time. Her words of wisdom and hope to those less-than-perfect humans like me have awakened my heart to the true holiness and grace of our great God. This book does more than enlighten . . . it changes the reader from the inside out. I thank God for Heather. Finally, someone brave enough to dismantle the wall of pride that keeps our eyes blinded. Finally, someone brave enough to bring us TRUTH."

—Priscilla Evans Shirer
Author of *A Jewel in His Crown*

"Heather Jamison's new book, *Reclaiming Intimacy*, is a powerful and important examination of an area often considered taboo among Christians. And yet it is an area that has a profound effect on many Christian marriages. Congratulations to Ms. Jamison for tackling such a difficult subject with honesty, sensitivity, and directness."

—Fred Holmes
Emmy award-winning writer and director

"This is a frank book, with penetrating honesty and abundant spiritual insight that cuts through lies that have led so many into premarital sex. If you're a single person, a married person who has had premarital sex, a parent of adolescents, or a pastor, *Reclaiming Intimacy* is a must-read."

—Gary Thomas
President of the Center for Evangelical Spirituality

"*Reclaiming Intimacy* reveals the personal cost of abandoning the sexual framework of the Bible, which transcends generational, cultural, or private preferences and points the way to recovery. Rid yourself of the spiritual and emotional debt incurred from self-gratification and begin revitalizing your marriage."

—Ramesh Richard, Ph.D., Th.D.
President, Ramesh Richard Evangelism and
Church Helps International
Professor, Dallas Theological Seminary

"Heather Jamison's book, *Reclaiming Intimacy*, stands as a superb example of how God often takes one's greatest point of brokenness and transforms it into his or her finest point of ministry. Drawing on her own experience, Jamison takes those who have misused the Creator's gift of sexual love and guides them back to authentic intimacy. In a culture that discounts sexual purity, this work stands like the one who called out to all who were too 'sophisticated' to see that 'The emperor isn't wearing any clothes!' As Jamison so ably shows, premarital sin mars and dents those it touches, but God is in the restoration business."

—Sandra Glahn
Coauthor of *Sexual Intimacy in Marriage*

"A rare book! Heather Jamison's vulnerability helps us grasp the devastation of a marriage founded on premarital sex and "cheap substitutes" for intimacy. Replete with Biblically-based remedies, Heather's book provides every person an answer for lonely isolation and a hope for beginning again."

— June Hunt
Host of "Hope for the Heart"

RECLAIMING
Intimacy

Overcoming the Consequences
of Premarital Relationships

Heather Jamison

kregel
PUBLICATIONS

Grand Rapids, MI 49501

Reclaiming Intimacy: Overcoming the Consequences of Premarital Relationships

© 2001 by Heather Jamison

Published by Kregel Publications, a division of Kregel, Inc., P.O. Box 2607, Grand Rapids, MI 49501.

Library of Congress Cataloging-in-Publication Data
Jamison, Heather.
    Reclaiming intimacy: overcoming the consequences of pre-marital relationships / Heather Jamison.
       p.   cm.
Includes bibliographical references.
    1. Premarital sex—Psychological aspects. 2. Sexual ethics. 3. Intimacy (Psychology). I. Title.
HQ31 .J33   2001   306.73—dc21   00-062942
                                      CIP

ISBN 978-0-8254-2940-8

Printed in the United States of America

5 6 7 8 / 12 11 10 09

It's difficult to dedicate something that is not mine, but I would like to ask You, Lord, to accept this book. I give it to You. Take what You already own and please bless it, break it, and multiply it. It is for Your glory only.

Contents

Foreword

If you feel insecure, separate, and alone, then you will relate to our story. I'm the male half of the equation in this story of premarital sex, and my experience is similar to Heather's. Like her, I looked for authentic intimacy, security, and acceptance in the counterfeit intimacy of premarital sex.

Reclaiming Intimacy not only identifies the problems of building true marital intimacy from the ruins of premarital sex, it outlines the solutions for fulfilling the legitimate longing that premarital sex only increases. And it does so with tact and honesty.

At this writing, Heather and I have been married for twelve years. We had been friends a few years before that. During this time I have sought fulfillment in many different things—baseball, academia, and money. None so wounded my future wife or me as did our involvement in premarital sex. In it we raised our own desires to an idolatrous level. Engaging in premarital sex provided only a false sense of intimacy, and I hurt the person whom I was supposed to love unselfishly—my bride-to-be.

Oswald Chambers said, "No love of the natural heart is safe unless it has been satisfied by God first." I have resolved to apply this truth to my marriage relationship. Attempts thus far have brought a depth of intimacy—with both God and Heather—that I had so desperately sought before in self-gratification.

There is nothing wrong with looking for love on earth—as long as we don't put our hope here. People, relationships, or material things can never be the source for the unfailing intimacy, security, and acceptance that only God can provide.

No matter how far you are on your journey, if you have traveled the wrong road in seeking to satisfy your longing for intimacy, if the road hasn't taken you where you'd hoped, if you want to learn to love better, this book can help you. *Reclaiming Intimacy* will give you new direction, new focus, and a new approach to living and loving with lasting intimacy.

—BRIAN JAMISON

Acknowledgments

I would like to thank the team at Kregel—Steve, Dennis, Janyre, and those whom I haven't become acquainted with but who have worked on this project. You are a professional group, but also very patient. Thank you.

Thank you, mom and dad, for providing me with a home of unconditional love. That foundation of acceptance frees me to be able to speak openly about my failures in the hope of helping others see God's grace more clearly.

Thank you, Gary Thomas, for the encouragement that you have given me, beginning some six years ago, to never give up on this idea. Thank you for validating the need for this book early on, when no one else seemed to agree.

Thank you, Dr. Cecil, for your selfless assistance and gracious encouragement.

Thank you, Dr. Al and Karen Cartmell, for opening your home to us while you were away and providing a refreshing place to work through the final stages of this book.

And to Sandi Glahn, thanks for everything—for introducing me to Kregel, for teaching me to write better, for making my sentences less boring. Thank you for the tips as well as the consolation. Thank you for always making time in your busy schedule to read rough drafts and help me smooth them out. Thank you for embracing this project when you have nothing to gain by it—this side of eternity—except a thank-you. You are a model of giving.

Brian, thank you. You went through this manuscript repeatedly, page by page and line by line, looking for theological accuracy and helping me to see when I wasn't so very clear. Thank you for beginning every suggested change with a compliment or three. I appreciate your acceptance, humor, and sensitivity. Thank you for taking my abstract and random thoughts and numerous pages of rough drafts and putting them all into a logical order. Thank you also for giving me "quiet times" to work on this project (with three children in our home, that sort of thing is a challenge). I could not have done this without your willingness to be vulnerable and open about our relationship in an effort to point others to Christ. You have been my biggest encourager, and you are my best friend.

Thank you, Lord. Your grace is the very air I breathe. Your faithfulness floods me entirely. Words could never do You justice, so I will end with the best description of all You are to me: *hikanotes*—my sufficiency.

Introduction

Recently Brian, our three children, and I watched the *Jesus* movie. It's a family favorite. Our four-year-old has rarely had the patience, though, to sit through it in its entirety. He usually ends up playing in his room before it is over.

This time, however, our son sat on my lap throughout the whole show. I wondered how he would react to the scenes of Jesus being crucified. Images of soldiers taking Jesus from the garden, beating Him, and spitting on Him hinted of the crucifixion to come. Our son watched intently. I held him close. On the television screen a soldier grasped his whip and lifted it. He was about to bring it down upon Jesus when our son could contain himself no longer. He screamed, "No! No! Don't do it! Don't do it! Don't do it!" He yelled the same thing later as the nails went into Jesus' hands. He quite made up his mind, when Jesus ascended into heaven, that Jesus left "because the people in that town were mean."

I've since wondered if our son's reaction isn't often played out in heaven, too. I imagine Jesus watching the ones He loves on His big-screen earth television. He watches the *Heather* movie or the *Brian* movie (or insert *your* name). He sees scenes of devotion to

Him. He sees scenes of devotion to ourselves. He sees us doing acts of obedience and thinking thoughts of affection. Then He sees us lured by the temptation of our flesh or by the deceit of the Evil One. He knows what will come next if we choose to sin. The images are offensive to His holiness. As we grasp the whip of self-will and raise it upon ourselves, He screams, "No! No! Don't do it! Don't do it! Don't do it!"

But we do.

I did. Perhaps you did too. We heard the faint cries of our Savior, but we blocked them out and continued in sin. Premarital sex is a particularly self-destructive sin, because it is committed against a person's own body. It is literally whipping oneself spiritually. When a Christian commits the act of premarital sex, he or she faces multiple consequences. One heavy consequence that shows up later is a lack of intimacy within what should be the most intimate relationship—marriage.

This book is about reclaiming the intimacy that was severed through the sin of premarital sex. I have written it because it is a topic that has not been addressed in Christian circles, and should be. Numerous books have been written about recovering from the effects of rape, incest, adultery—all devastating offenses, to be sure. The damage from engaging in premarital sex, however, affects a far greater number of people, albeit in a far less visible way. To the Christian community, premarital sex is the elephant under the rug. We hide it under layers of silence; we tread carefully around it. We know the elephant is there, but such a beast seems too much to contend with so we leave it alone—ignored and accountable only to itself.

Christians don't talk about premarital sex because we are ashamed to admit that many of us have engaged in it. Admitting that we have had premarital sex means admitting to being undisciplined, disobedient, and pleasure seeking. We'd rather others didn't know that about us. We want to save face. But because I hope to save a face far greater than mine, I write this book without the shield of anonymity.

You see, I am a sinner saved by grace—the totally unmerited favor from God. There is no reason for God to have anything to do with me. There is no reason for Him to restore the relationship between my husband and me. But He did anyway. He called me. I ran away. He forgave. I returned, only to run away again. He chastised me. I ran even farther. He kept calling. He kept forgiving. He kept chastising. He gave grace.

For that reason, I want to paint a complete portrait of His grace in order to give hope for those who struggle with the consequences of past sexual sin. For me to remain anonymous because of shame would be to spit on the cross of Jesus in the name of false pride. Hiding behind anonymity suggests that Jesus' death covers some sins, but not all. It implies that I am susceptible to some sins, but not to all.

In truth, I am a sinner—totally. Jesus' blood cleansed me—completely. His power freed me. His love fills me. I speak openly about my sin and salvation in order to show you the glory of the face of Jesus.

In writing a book about my sin of premarital sex, however, I am not writing solely about myself. Brian has given his support to and ongoing help on this project. But I tell this story only after first accepting full responsibility for my actions. My sin is just that—mine—and reflects on me only.

To better convey the nature of the sin of premarital sex and its consequences, this book is divided into three sections. The first section deals with the desire for achieving intimacy. While the quest is legitimate, we often give in to influences that encourage us toward fulfilling it through counterfeit means—premarital sex. Engaging in premarital sex, however, creates challenges to authentic intimacy. Section two walks through some of those challenges. Section three focuses on reclaiming or even creating marital intimacy in a relationship that has been adversely affected by engaging in premarital sex. The topics covered in section three do not appear in most self-help books. They are unique to the wounds created by sexual sin. The self-help steps deal more with the heart than with outward actions, but I have found them to be lasting in effect. Actions follow the heart, however, so the heart is a good place to begin.

In St. Augustine's *Confessions,* the fourth-century priest told of things that had shamed and burdened his soul. In an effort to knock himself off of the pedestal that many in his day had placed him on, Augustine revealed personal details of his life. He also wrote so that readers could identify with the spiritual tensions he had faced. Although readers might not have struggled with St. Augustine's precise temptations or sins, they could apply the lessons he had learned to their own lives. I relate my own experience for the same reason—so that readers can apply the lessons I learned to their own lives.

In his *Confessions,* Augustine wrote about stealing fruit from a neighbor's tree. He was not hungry, but his delight in stealing the fruit came simply from taking something that was not his. I stole intimacy from a person I now dearly love—Brian. I could not have truly loved him at the time, because my very action of premarital sex with him was dishonoring. I was desirous of Brian in the same way that Augustine was of the fruit. And, like Augustine, I stole for the sheer pleasure of doing so.

Reclaiming Intimacy reveals the emptiness that comes from self-gratification. It is written to serve as a companion for those who wish to walk the road from sexual sin to relational healing.

I don't have a perfect marriage. But I do have a marriage that is better now than I ever thought possible. I have a husband who loves me even when I'm unlovable. And I have a heart to honor him with my life.

Still, why should you listen to me? A Christian lady, whom I admire, offered me this counsel,

> Dearest Heather, I know you have heard it said many times that the Christian life is one beggar telling another beggar where to find food. You do not have to have a perfectly resolved relationship to deeply minister to others through what you've experienced. You can share the journey. . . . Two sinners married to each other. . . . You are broken and His grace will be shown through your weakness.

What I have learned, I offer to you. Where I have applied the concepts of this book in my own marriage, I have seen intimacy restored and our relationship deepened. By joining me on my quest for intimacy you may see that your own quest has similarly led you astray from the True Source of intimacy. If the intimacy in your marriage has been shattered by memories of premarital sexual relationships, you can reclaim that intimacy. Your marriage can be strengthened so that it can become a vessel of ministry for God's kingdom.

Whatever I say, however, will have little value without a personal relationship with Jesus Christ. He has the answers; He has the power. He is love; He is intimacy. Without the Author of authentic intimacy, marital intimacy will be no better than a clever forgery. Mine was for many years. But, by God's grace, intimacy has been reclaimed and continues to mature.

Section 1

The Quest for Intimacy

1

Losing My Way

"Why aren't you crying?" Brian said. "Why aren't you crying?" It was more an accusation than a question. He slammed the car door, leaving me alone behind the steering wheel. He then walked about twenty feet and sat down on the curb.

A few hours earlier I sat in the doctor's office thumbing through teen magazines. While I flipped the pages, my thoughts raced to plans for the college fraternity dance that night. I had a tanning appointment to keep. I debated whether to wear a shawl or be a slave to style and freeze. My stomach grumbled because I'd skipped lunch so I could squeeze more easily into my size-three, black velvet dress.

This doctor's appointment had inconvenienced me. On top of that, the office was running behind schedule, and I had grown impatient. In fact, that's why I was visiting the doctor. I'd grown impatient waiting for my monthly cycle to begin. My mom said I should see her doctor and made an appointment for me. Mom suspected that I might have endometriosis, a disease that infects the female reproductive system. Women who have never been pregnant are at a higher risk for developing endometriosis, which often causes infertility.

So on the eve of my doctor's appointment, I had sat somberly with Brian, brooding over pamphlets on endometriosis. "I'm sorry," I said.

"What for?" he asked.

"If I do have endometriosis," I said, "then I might not ever be able to have children."

He gave me a gentle squeeze and mumbled, "That's okay. I'll still love you." I commended myself for having such a noble and understanding boyfriend.

Waiting in the doctor's office, I thought about the home pregnancy test I'd bought with money from my eighteenth birthday. It had turned up negative. I'd run the test to be certain I wasn't pregnant before telling my mom I was late with my period. I'd kept track of the number of times Brian and I had had sex. I knew the chances I could be pregnant were slight. As a freshman in college with my whole life ahead of me—or at least a night of dancing—pregnancy wasn't an option. Besides, what would my parents say?

I was their youngest and attended church regularly. My father had served actively as a deacon and taught youth Sunday school while I was growing up. My mother, a teacher and leader for Bible Study Fellowship, guided women through studies on the Bible. We had lived just two houses down from our church during that time, and we wore a path between its front door and ours.

As a child, I remember saying the sinner's prayer several times for good measure. I could name the books of the Bible and retell most Bible stories to boot. I figured that God was happy just to have me on His team. I didn't drink, do drugs, smoke, or swear. Unfortunately, that wasn't all I didn't do. I didn't know God. I suppose I didn't want to know Him—not if it meant giving up something . . . anything.

While I knew there was a God, I refused to acknowledge Him as God. I thought up fanciful ideas of what God was like. The

God I imagined was busy controlling the universe, molding the mountains, and directing the seas. He had parted the oceans, painted the rainbows, and planted the trees. Why would He be concerned with me? I had convinced myself that God had better things to do than keep track of me. As a result, the line between right and wrong turned into a hyphen. I traded my Bible for a boy, my prayers for a party, and my purity for a person.

If I were pregnant, I wondered, *how would Brian react?* I was an honor roll student, accustomed to invoking approval. As a cheerleader and pom-pom girl, I often received praise and applause. What could I expect if I was pregnant? I doubted that Brian would applaud. What would my friends say? What about my pastor? Or my grandparents? My siblings? What about Brian's friends? What would Brian's parents say?

In high school, Brian had served as the president of his church youth group. He was inducted into the National Honor Society and chosen by teachers to serve as a peer counselor for our campus. He was the slugging leader on the varsity baseball team and an all-district football player as well. Brian held the record for the most rushing touchdowns in a season. In a small town like ours, Brian's athletic record elevated him to near Herculean status.

Now a sophomore in college on an athletic scholarship Brian had hopes of pursuing a professional baseball career. Like me, he didn't drink, do drugs, smoke, or swear. In fact, Brian took it one step further than I—he didn't even hang around people who did. Image. It was everything.

But for Brian and me that image now floated in a specimen cup.

"You're pregnant." The nurse's voice sounded as sterile as the examining room. I stared ahead. It would have been easier if I hadn't known her. It would have been easier if she hadn't gone to my church. It would have been easier if her family hadn't been friends with my folks.

"Are you going to be okay?" she asked. I knew she had battled with infertility and eventually had adopted. How odd she must have felt consoling me for being pregnant.

"Yes, we'll be fine." I plastered a smile onto my face, feeling like the Cheshire cat from *Alice in Wonderland.* I would have preferred, like the cat, to disappear.

"You're pregnant." Her words echoed down in the pit of my stomach.

Reared in a Christian home, surrounded by Christian principles, I never thought I would be pregnant before I married. On the outside I was a squeaky-clean Christian, and no one would ever have known or suspected what I had done. But God saw the inside, and He knew. He knew all along.

God had been long-suffering and patient through the early months when Brian and I were having sex. During that time, the suppressed guilt and the knowledge that engaging in sex was wrong remained tucked in the corner of my mind. The lure of stolen moments was like a cable, pulling me up and up on a roller-coaster ride. I heard the echo of screams, those who had gone before me, yet I felt too enthralled with the breathtaking view and the tantalizing ascent to fear the inevitable fall. Now God's safety belt had disappeared. I'd crested the top and lurched forward as my descent propelled me upside-down and in circles.

Months earlier when the ride began, I had gazed at Brian much like Alice gazed into the looking glass. *What happens if I go ahead?* I wondered. *Would it be so bad?* It seemed as if everybody else was doing it. Popular songs such as "I Want Your Sex," MTV videos, television shows, and teen magazine advertisements sold free sex as natural.

And I belong to Generation X, 82 percent of whom have had sex by the age of nineteen.[1] I studied in schools where ACT scores are among the highest in the world, and where positive pregnancy tests rank near the top among industrialized nations. I lived in the Bible Belt where it is assumed that Sunday school is a natural complement to public education.

Yet I made the mistake of basing my personal belief system on outward behavior and accolades. I went to church, correctly answered all the questions in Sunday school, and didn't wear rebellious clothing. But my relationship with Jesus seemed no more real than Alice's illusion of a talking white rabbit. Of course, I knew who Jesus was, and if anyone had asked I would have said I believed in Him.

But in Bible Belt, middle-class America, assenting to Christianity is akin to assenting to being alive or residing in Missouri or liking baseball. The seeds of faith fell into shallow soil, and choked by the sin and selfishness that is my nature, a true knowledge of Jesus did not take root.

A few months into my sexual activity, I confided in an older friend, who was a virgin. She stared at me a moment and said, "Are you just plain dumb?"

Was I? Are the millions of people, who consider themselves Christians while having premarital sex, dumb? Perhaps. But in retrospect, I think deceived might be a better term. I was deceived, that is, by my own selfishness and sinfulness. True, we all have a need and a desire for closeness with another individual, but selfishness and sinfulness clouded my senses and lowered my defenses. And everywhere there were cultural, psychological, and physiological influences that encouraged and supported my self-deception.

Modern society has become a breeding ground for premarital sex. A misguided sense of tolerance and a permissive pop culture have created an environment ripe for it. Chief among the things that influence young people to have sex too soon are its easy accessibility, the media's glamorizing of it, and peer pressure.

Accessibility

Teenagers have always engaged in sexual relations, but the last two decades in America have brought the greatest increase ever in accessibility. The pursuit of economic prosperity has led to more two-wage-earner families, resulting in latchkey kids. More mothers working outside the home mean smaller families and the disintegration of the typical nuclear family. Where once families spent leisure time together, today each family member is likely to be engaged in separate recreational activities. Thus, the American teenager is literally *Home Alone*.

"I trust my son," one mother said not long ago on national television. "There are condoms in every room of our house."[2] This woman's trust obviously rested in her son's ability to practice "safe sex," not in his maturity to use self-control.

Not only do some parents offer their kids condoms or birth control pills, but many teens have private bedrooms and their own cars. Many state colleges and universities have adopted coed dorms and a number of dorms offer coed floors. Teens also often have private recreational areas, lofts, or basements.

During my freshman year in college, for instance, I lived in a basement room rather than on campus. I had a private bath and almost exclusive access to an entertainment room. Brian roomed with a boy on the college campus and had no curfew or accountability for his whereabouts. This being so, Brian spent many hours with me. We were not unlike many of the teenagers we knew who, for all intents and purposes, lived together while dating.

It's true that teenagers are creative and determined. They need only a parked car and an abandoned lot to accomplish their goal. But easy accessibility to both privacy and contraceptives does nothing to discourage active adolescent hormones.

Media Glamorizing

When I was in high school, the television show *Moonlighting* topped the charts. Other than a chased criminal here or there, the subplot each week consisted of whether or not Maddie, the female detective, would ever have sex with David Addison, her male counterpart.

Brian loved the show so much he wrote his junior term paper on it. We watched *Moonlighting* religiously every Thursday night. *Moonlighting* is only one example out of the plethora of popular, sensually provocative television programming. Brian and I also watched MTV together late at night. You can, no doubt, fill in the blanks.

That was over a decade ago, and media glamorizing of unmarried sex merely simmered then. Today it boils over onto America's youth and its singles population.

- "Of the fifty-eight shows monitored by *U.S. News and World Report*, almost half contained sexual acts or references to sex."
- The same study also concluded that sexual activity or innuendo took place, on average, every four minutes during the prime-time hours.[3]
- A more recent study by the Henry J. Kaiser Family Foundation found that 56 percent of the 1,351 shows sampled and two-thirds of prime-time ones had sexual content.[4]

Media studies always arrive at the same conclusion: The media influence people.

Billionaire and television-giant Ted Turner acknowledges that "everything we're exposed to influences us . . . films influence us, and the TV programs we see influence us. The weaker your family is, the more they influence *you*."[5]

Most secular magazines that today's teens have easy access to feature sexual language, painting the picture that *everyone* is doing it. Although the articles aren't often blatantly titled "Ten Techniques to a Better Sex Life," sometimes they are. Consider the recent article entitled "Cosmo Confessions,"[6] in which readers speak openly about their steamiest sexual experiences, or "Glamour's Super Sex Challenge,"[7] in which readers were challenged to have sex daily for thirty days and then tell about it. For the most part, however, magazines influence young minds through a subtle yet pervasive message that glamorizes unmarried sex. Following a fight just "kiss and make out, er . . . make up," wrote one woman in a recent teen article on boyfriend/girlfriend relationships.[8]

The media's picture of relationships is colored by the allure of physical contact. Most teens do not have the spiritual or emotional maturity to recognize a clever forgery of authentic intimacy.

Peer Pressure

One evening during high school, my friends and I huddled in a circle at pom-pom camp, doing what most girls do—giggle, tell stories, and talk. When the topic turned to sex, I grew uncomfortable. I had just recently moved to this new high school, and I didn't yet have the time-sealed loyalty and sense of belonging for which I yearned.

From previous conversations, I knew that most of the girls claimed they had had sex. The same was true at my former school on another squad. What I didn't know and soon learned was that, with the exception of myself and one other girl, Sarah, they *all* claimed to have had it.

Sarah was a confident Christian who showed no hesitation in endorsing virginity. I, on the other hand, lied. "Yeah, I've done it," I said, not offering any details. The conversation returned to the other girls, who shared their accomplishments in explicit language. I slid off the hot seat—but only temporarily. I soon burned with guilt.

I felt guilty because I had lied, but also because I had belittled Sarah's position and abandoned her. When, months later, I was sexually tempted, I figured since I had blown it verbally already I had one less reason to say no.

"Premarital sex is so common in our culture today that some people are considered old-fashioned, if not prudish, for maintaining their purity until marriage," writes one marriage preparation book.[9] Thus, those who do maintain their purity may not feel comfortable even admitting it. Recently, while attending a conference, I began talking with a lady. She must have misunderstood something I said, for she suddenly shrieked, grabbed my hands, and asked, "You're a virgin, too?" She was about to hug me when, although I hated to dampen her excitement, I told her I wasn't.

She then said, somewhat embarrassed at her previous reaction, "Oh, I'm so sorry. You have to understand that there aren't that many of us, and when I find another virgin, I'm thrilled. We have to stick together." The number of virgins is relatively few today. They may sense pressure to conform simply in the sheer absence of peer support.

Although peer support for virginity is sorely lacking, peer pressure to have sex comes in many forms. It appears outright as a challenge, or it surfaces in a confrontational way. It even comes clothed as a caring friend. For females, peer pressure is probably not as blatant, but it remains present. For males, sexual activity is often viewed as a trophy captured on one's way to manhood.

Often, however, the most coercive peer pressure comes from the boy or girl within a dating relationship. Statements like, "If you really loved me you would want to make me happy," or "We're going to get married anyhow," annihilate standards and lower resistance.

Youth writer and speaker Josh McDowell states, "Peer pressure as it operates among today's teens sometimes becomes a kind of 'moral blackmail.' The basis for this blackmail is the group's power to accept or reject. . . . Even Christian teens, who have grown up with biblical morality, find themselves discarding or ignoring those values because of their fear of rejection."[10] Teens give in to pressure on a date, then, not because they're afraid of incurring the anger of a girlfriend or boyfriend. What they're really afraid of is being rejected. Refusing intimacy does not lead to hate—it leads to loneliness. And loneliness is conceived in rejection.

While cultural influences and one's peers create external motives to give in to one's desires, psychological and physiological influences attack teens from the inside. The human need for love and acceptance, the desire to escape relationship problems and, to be blunt, the fact that sex feels good all exert their own pressures.

Human Need for Love and Acceptance

A 1950s book, *Facts of Life and Love for Teenagers,* instructs young girls who find that their dates' hands "begin to wander into the no-man's-land" to remove the hand. The girl should then say with surprise, "Why, this isn't Tuesday, is it?" If that doesn't work, struggle "free of his embrace, [shake your] curls with a jerky laugh," and say, "Ooooh, please, you are too much for me." Or there is always the tactic of turning the key in the ignition and sweetly asking, "Will you drive, or shall I?"[11]

All three responses might have been properly understood in the 1950s, but today play out as teasing. While advances and responses may change over time, a desire for acceptance and love remains the same.

"Getting a boy to stop his love-making is hard for some girls," this same 1950s book records. "They are so hungry for loving that they cling to any expression of affection that they can evoke. Girls may be so afraid of losing the boy's attention that they dare not refuse him intimacies that he seems to enjoy."[12]

Underneath any peer pressure and media influence lies a person's desire for acceptance. Remove this element, and much of what exists in the media and with friends would have little affect on one's behavior.

Present within each of us is an innate desire to belong. Our need for intimacy is as natural as our need for air. Prior to sin entering the world, Adam and Eve experienced a perfect relationship with God. After eating the forbidden fruit, they hid from God. In so doing, they tried to separate themselves from God when, in fact, their sin had already done so.

Restoring the intimate relationship between a person and God requires a grace that many people doubt exists. So we often attempt to circumvent intimacy with God through relationships with other people. We give ourselves sexually to others in the hope of securing love, acceptance, and intimacy.

"We all want to be someone's hero or someone's beauty, to be in a relationship of heroic proportions. Contrary to legalistic forms of self-denial, we need to feel free to admit this without embarrassment,"[13] writes Brent Curtis and John Eldredge in the *Sacred Romance*. Sex serves as a counterfeit means to a legitimate desire. But the firecrackers that explode during the first few months of illicit sexual activity dull and fade with time.

A history teacher at the high school where I used to teach uses firecrackers during his lecture on Nazi Germany. The exploding firecrackers illustrate how people become desensitized to violence through repetitive exposure. The teacher inconspicuously lights his firecrackers and drops the bundle into his metal trash can. He then sits back to watch the show.

On the first series of explosions, the kids nearly hit the ceiling, jumping out of their chairs and scattering in all directions. Their faces grow pale. Their pulses pound. When the kids recognize the cause of the commotion they settle back into their chairs. They remain perplexed but no longer startled. The noise echoes, but no one stirs. By the last pop and fizzle, they are all laughing.

Like the diminishing effects of the firecrackers on the students, illicit sex, too, loses its intensity over time. It derives much of its excitement from the exhilaration of feeling love and acceptance. When the love and acceptance grow commonplace, they become less valuable. We question if the feelings of our partners are sincere. Without the security of committed love, the firecrackers of a passionate relationship begin to fizzle under familiarity and burn out under contempt.

Escaping Relationship Problems

Early in our sexual relationship Brian had an argument with a family member. Arguments are not unusual; teenagers often argue with family members. But hurt feelings within a close relationship like family can propel intense emotions. Brian came to me. I took pity on him. We got carried away. How many times has that scenario played out on the stage of Christian America?

Sex acts as an anodyne, relieving pain or at least numbing it for a while. In turning to illicit sex, people try temporarily to escape any number of family stresses. Dysfunction, incest, dominance, absent parenting, and physical or verbal abuse exist in a large number of homes. Not all families experience severe problems, but no home is perfect. We are sinners living in a sinful world. Whether at home, school, work, or even in recreational activities, everyone experiences disappointments in relationships. What we do with these disappointments either pushes us to God—our "Totally Other"—or to other people, totally broken like ourselves.

What we often do not see, however, in premarital sexual relationships is the brokenness of the object of our desire. Rather, the other person is viewed as a healer to our relational woes. The close feel of someone else's arms seems to engulf the empty hole caused by relational friction. Touch sensations distract feelings of rejection, loneliness, or fear. A heart is venerated through the intrinsic value of providing pleasure to oneself or another.

The pleasure of being the center, even momentarily, of somebody's universe can numb even the strongest emotional pain. Yet when the numbness lifts, the quest for authentic intimacy continues.

Sex Feels Good

Statistics and psychological studies aside, when it comes down to it, sex is just plain fun. Add to it the illicit pleasure of doing something forbidden and sinful, and the result is a delicious yet disastrous temptation.

Dr. Willard Harley, the psychologist and counselor of *His Needs, Her Needs* fame, referred to the allure of forbidden fruit in a recent conversation with me. "Some of the best sexual relationships," he said, "are adulterous. The night they get married, it's over."[14] Harley neglected to mention, however, the frequency with which couples who abstain from premarital or extramarital sex report a deep level of intimacy in combination with great sex. Instead of beginning with sex, they have first communicated and laid a foundation for a healthy relationship.

Even so, most unmarried teenagers don't realize that married sex can be great sex, nor do they believe it. Why should they? Youth pastors and Christian leaders rarely speak openly about God's blessing of sex. But even if they did, most Christian teens have not been trained in developing the patience to wait until marriage for sex. So the forbidden fruit combined with the raging hormones of adolescents—who perceive unhappy married couples plagued with emotional emptiness—creates a prescription for disaster.

Sex is a natural desire—some would say, need. Torrents of testosterone propel young men toward one goal. Mid-cycle estrogen provides eager partners. Natural desires dominate decisions about love.

"One of the cruelest ways to kill natural love," writes Oswald Chambers, "is through the rejection that results from having built that love on natural desires."[15] Natural desires diminish with time leaving no foundation for a relationship that is meant to last a lifetime. Sure, sex feels good but so does a warm fire on a cold winter day—as long as the fire stays inside the fireplace. Sex outside of a marriage relationship is like a fire gone wild. It will burn. It will scar. That is its nature.

Any of a myriad of cultural, psychological, and physiological influences can play into a person's decision to engage in premarital sex. Humans are intricate beings, created by a passionate and loving God. We possess the ability to love, to hate, to desire—and to reason. When trying to discover the motives for engaging in unmarried sex, we can rarely pinpoint a single reason. A combination of influences—events, conversations, relationships—affect our choices.

Pointing fingers at peers, parents, movies, music, and clothes only shows how high we can count. Claiming that changing one thing or another will make a behavior disappear naively dismisses the one critical fact—that we are fallen creatures hell-bent on sinning. God gives the desire to overcome temptation; the Holy Spirit provides the strength to do so. Without the daily work of the Spirit in a person's life, chastity remains the exception rather than the rule.

"Why aren't you crying?" Brian's question echoed in my mind as I sat in my car and replayed the circumstances and unwise decisions that had brought me to this point. I had violated God's design for marriage when I, like Alice, stepped through the look-ing glass into what I thought would be a wonderland. But my wonderland had gone mad. And intimacy now lay shattered like a broken mirror.

2

My True Longing

Brian still sat on the curb, his head lowered in despair.

I wasn't about to drive away though, no matter how long he sat there and no matter what he said. I needed him. After all, *I* didn't have a problem—*we* did. Three hours remained until the dinner and dance. Both sets of parents would soon be eagerly waiting at my house to see us off. My parents, however, had scheduled a weekend trip and were to leave the next morning. That would give us some time to figure out what to do. If we could just make it through that night.

As I sat in the car, I thought that Brian's question was perhaps a good question. Why wasn't I crying? My life, as I knew it, had vanished. The outward appearance of my innocence would now be gone. My own actions had torn me out of the world of Friday night football games and drop-kicked me headfirst into the real world. Wasn't that worth a few tears?

I supposed so. But by then I had run out. Tears had flowed freely on the twenty-minute drive from the doctor's office to my home. Niagara burst forth when, at a stoplight, I pulled up behind a former cheerleader and classmate who, six months earlier, had gotten pregnant and then married. I had inwardly condemned her when it happened. Judge not lest . . .

By now, though, I had settled into shock, too numb for tears. And I would need to be numb to get through the evening. Brian finally came back to the car, and we agreed to go ahead with the dance. We later posed for the cameras while both sets of parents complimented each other on what a nice couple we were turning out to be.

The dance dragged on uneventfully. We watched the others dance and talk. Then we left early. The weekend didn't give us nearly enough time to think. On Monday we told my parents. Their disappointment was veiled by compassion and encouragement and offers of support.

Next, we told Brian's parents. A meeting of the two families was called.

There we were, Brian and I sitting on the floor. What little maturity we had diminished under the stress, and we behaved like kids being punished. Choices were played out before us like cards dealt onto the table. Adoption. Marriage. Engagement. Single parenthood. Abortion was never considered.

If we got married, it would need to be soon. It was December, and Christmas was fast approaching. Brian and I didn't want to disrupt the holidays with a rushed wedding. And, since I was early on in the pregnancy, it was thought that maybe we could hide our infraction by leaving as much time as possible between the wedding and the birth of our baby. Maybe the dates wouldn't betray our secret.

Right. I doubted that people in our small town would be so naive to think that I got pregnant on my honeymoon. But my head was spinning, and I remained silent while emotions somersaulted in my heart.

So I nodded in agreement. Brian did too. The wedding would

take place in nine days. We scheduled it for a Friday evening following our college final exams. After the wedding, we would have a weekend for a local honeymoon and still have a week before Christmas.

I turned to Brian for support but saw only a fragile boy who had been taken to the woodshed. He saw a treat gone sour. We were weak. We were sinful. Our infatuation with one another had hidden these things before. And now we were broken.

Rather than turn to God for help and healing, we continued to look to what our counterfeit intimacy had trained us to look to . . . each other. This brought only disappointment and, later, anger. I, along with many other teens, had used unmarried sex as a misguided effort to meet the legitimate longing for intimacy. Sensing the need inside, I had tried to fill it with a tangible relationship. What I didn't realize was that all people are sinners, and no one could meet my need for total acceptance and love except God.

But why do we have these longings? Why do we quest after intimacy? If we are believers in Christ, why hasn't God filled us?

We experience longing because of separation. Following Adam's sin, God transplanted mankind like embryos, out of a perfect womb—the garden—and into a test tube of sorts—the world. Sin had separated our spirit from the One who fed it. The opportunity for an unhindered relationship with the Father had ceased. And just as no amount of ingeniousness or persistence on the part of humans can recreate the flawless nurture a child receives in the womb, neither can physical gratification or emotional stimulus fill the hollow that results from living as a sinner separated from God.

Without the ability to relate perfectly to God, we often try to fulfill our longings with other things. We act like a vining plant. Outside the office window in the house where we used to live I experimented one spring to see if a vining plant would climb the bricks around the window frame. Despite my best efforts, even giving it nails to hang on, without being able to wrap itself around the bricks, the vine could not climb. It remained on the ground and lacked flowers even when it was past time for it to bloom.

A vining plant instinctively knows, however, it ought to climb. So when a weed grew near it, the vine wrapped itself around the weed and climbed that, sometimes going almost two feet off the ground. It grew only so high, however, and then it would topple over, lacking the support structure to sustain its weight.

God designed us with a longing to climb toward heaven. He has set eternity in our hearts. We lack the ability, however, to climb there on our own. Sensing the need, we often climb weeds instead—pleasure, ambition, giftedness, or relationships—and as a result we never bloom. These weeds also include imperfect human love. While providing temporary delight at best, imperfect human love remains imperfect and unable to provide the proper strength and support.

We long, too, because of the curse. After Adam and Eve's sin, God pronounced a curse on them. And we continue to long, because we live in a cursed environment. It's only when we climb upward in the love of God that we flourish.

Christian counselor Dr. Larry Crabb explains, "Ever since God expelled Adam and Eve from the garden, we have lived in an unnatural environment, a world in which we were not designed to live. We were *built* to enjoy a garden without weeds, relationships without friction, fellowship without distance."[1]

Before the fruit and the snake, humankind's desire naturally stretched toward God. Real desire rose, rightly directed. Perfect intimacy and connection thrived in the bosoms of the created. Yet sin severed the bond.

As a result of the curse, the woman's desire was turned from God toward man. "To the woman He said, 'I will greatly multiply your pain in childbirth, in pain you shall bring forth children; yet

your *desire* shall be for your husband, and he shall rule over you'"
(Gen. 3:16, emphasis added).

More can be learned about the meaning of this verse by looking
at the original Hebrew. *Desire* here comes from the Hebrew word
teshuqah. *Teshuqah* is defined as a "stretching out after; a longing."[2]
A woman's longing stretches out after the man. In context, it can be
seen that the longing on the part of the woman is not a mere flirta-
tious hoping for affection but a desire for rule or control.

More can sometimes be learned about the meaning of a word in
its original language by comparing it to the way it is used in other
places in the Bible. The word *teshuqah* is used in only two other
places in Scripture. Genesis 4:7 uses *teshuqah* when God tells Cain
that sin is "crouching at the door, and its desire *(teshuqah)* is for"
him. It continues by saying that Cain should master, or "rule," it.
This supports *teshuqah* being used in Genesis 3:16 to suggest a
desire for rule.

It is interesting that Cain chooses not to "rule" it and instead
succumbs to it by killing his brother, Abel. So the Lord punishes
Cain. For the rest of his life, the ground that Cain tills will be
barren. For failing to "rule" over sin as God told him to, Cain
suffers two consequences—death and devastation. Similarly, when
a marriage relationship does not reflect God's design for authority,
it too suffers consequences.

The only other location of *teshuqah* in Scripture is, ironically, in
the Bible's book on sex—the Song of Songs. The married woman
speaks, "I am my beloved's, and his *desire [teshuqah]* is for me"
(Song 7:10, emphasis added).

One commentator notes, "[This passage from Song of Songs] is
as if we are observing the Fall momentarily reversed. It obviously
is a strong, almost overpowering, urge. His desire for her easily
equals hers for him. She is at no disadvantage."[3]

In the world after the curse, however, a woman's sexuality carries a lot of weight with regard to her partner. Within a relationship based primarily on sex, desire is mutual, but rule is interchangeable—and sexual influence carries power. Ask Samson. His desire for Delilah cost him everything.

The woman's desire *(teshuqah)* for man sometimes makes her misuse her sexual power. She may offer herself through premarital sex, using it as a playing card for maintaining or dictating a relationship.

As a young girl infatuated with an older, college athlete, I obviously didn't possess the control in our relationship. Not, that is, until we began to have sex. Then the reins of control changed quickly in the relationship, and I gained the upper hand. At the time, I didn't understand the power of sexual dynamics, but when I had secured control of Brian's devotion my infatuation quite predictably diminished, and my interests turned elsewhere. Such is the irony of control.

Another result of the original curse, though, is that God says the man shall "rule" over the woman. Scholars interpret this in a variety of ways. Yet, most will agree that, at the least, "rule" means "authority." Any time women step outside of God's prescribed program and offer our bodies to gain "authority" over men, we are in disobedience, and this ultimately leads—as it did with Cain, who did not rule sin—to devastation. Devastation may take the forms of contempt, distrust, and resentment. If a woman plays the premarital sex card in a *desire* to "rule" her man, then she has not only disobeyed God's law on purity but also His will on authority. In cases of multilevel sin, myriad consequences result.

Consider what happens if a woman carries into marriage the pattern of using her body to control the relationship. It may become difficult for her husband to lead wisely. If the husband succumbs to his wife, they both experience difficulty in the relationship. The apostle James writes, "But each one is tempted when he is carried away and enticed by his own lust. Then when lust has conceived, it

gives birth to sin; and when sin is accomplished, it brings forth death"
(James 1:14–15).

Premarital sex, then, can lay the groundwork for a barren, dry,
or even dead marriage relationship. Efforts to establish marital intimacy must begin with acknowledging how and why our quest
for authentic intimacy first took us astray.

We have a legitimate longing for wholeness because we are separated from God, and we live in a cursed environment. Because of
the fall, we may try to meet our legitimate longing for wholeness
through someone other than God, all the while forgetting the frailty
and limitations of the flesh.

Blaise Pascal, the brilliant French mathematician and orthodox
Christian, once said that there is a God-shaped hole inside everyone that can only be filled by God. A popular children's songwriter
refers to it as the hole in the middle of a doughnut. We often seek
to fill that hole, but we can't. God gave us the longing to fill that
hole in order to draw us to Him. It is our truest longing. The
longing itself is not wrong, but what we choose to do with that
longing is often wrong.

"Pleasure, money, power, and safety are all, as far as they go,
good things," writes C. S. Lewis. "The badness consists in pursuing them by the wrong method. . . . wickedness, when you examine it, turns out to be the pursuit of some good in the wrong way."[4]
Unmarried sex, when you examine it, is the pursuit of spiritual
wholeness in the wrong way.

After having counseled countless numbers of sexually active teenagers, youth minister Bob Bartlett says,

> I began to realize . . . that they were looking for something
> that was good and holy. They just didn't do it the right
> way. They were after intimacy, but they tried to take the
> shortcut of sex. . . . They tried for the instant gratification,

which our society is so good at, and they found it didn't
get them what they wanted. . . . They were looking for
someone to connect with.[5]

An example of people looking for wholeness or someone to
connect with is the recent doctrine called "spiritual connections."
In a large church in the Northwest, the pastor twisted legitimate
human longing into something sordid. After teaching truth—
that one's spouse couldn't meet all of one's needs—the pastor
then encouraged his congregation to fulfill their unmet needs by
"connecting" with other people's spouses. These "spiritual connections" came through intimate dancing, kissing, and in some
cases sex. Thousands of lives crumbled while divorces, suicides,
and even murder plagued the church before its inevitable de-
mise.[6] So-called "spiritual connections" turned out to be nothing more than sin. Rather than looking to God to fill the
"God-shaped hole" inside, these church members looked to
earthly solutions.

The members of that Northwest church no doubt seemed to be
active Christians, just as Brian and I had. And they, like Brian and
I, no doubt rationalized their behavior so they would feel comfortable about it. But filling the longing for God with the wrong
contents is like pouring Kool-Aid into your gas tank. Your car
looks nice on the outside, it feels comfortable on the inside, but it
won't run—no matter how much Kool-Aid you pour in, and no
matter what flavor you use.

Crabb sums it up this way: "We long for the satisfaction we
were built to enjoy, but we all move away from God to find it. . . .
We don't want to accept the fact that, since the Fall, *no* human
being has the capacity to love us perfectly."[7]

And so, in reaching for authentic intimacy we, like vining plants,
often climb weeds. When the weeds take the form of human love,

we topple under the weight of our own disillusionment. In a marriage built on counterfeit intimacy, lack of trust and respect, regret, shame, doubt, guilt, resentment, and anger are often not immediately apparent. Thus the connection between cause and effect may not be immediately apparent, leaving us unsure why our marriages, like the vine, have not bloomed. Such marriages not only fail to bloom, but they may actually become diseased.

Marriages do not, of course, consist of flowers and blooms. Marriage is an institution of human beings who are capable of bearing wounds from embattled relationships. When a person suffers a physical wound, such as a knife cut, tetanus may result from unchecked bacteria. For the first three to four days, the person shows no symptoms of tetanus. Then he or she becomes a little stiff. The jaw holds its place, and after a few more days muscles begin to spasm. In a few weeks, the entire body spasms continually. Twenty-five percent of those who contract tetanus die from suffocation within a month.

Marital relationships wounded by sexual manipulation may show no symptoms for the first few years. But then the relationship becomes a little rigid, a little formal. Both spouses become stiff-necked. After a few years, the relationship experiences spasms—knee-jerk reactions dictated by emotion rather than will. Fights get out of hand. With enough spasms, enough fights, enough stiff-necked opposition, the relationship suffocates and dies.

Tetanus is a highly treatable disease. Death occurs only when people do not realize the severity of their initial wound and do not take the necessary steps to treat it. Likewise, many couples do not recognize why their relationships are showing signs of infection and weakness. They assume they have simply fallen out of love.

Couples rarely seek professional counseling when they think they've fallen out of love. *We're not going to go to a counselor just because she doesn't light my fire anymore,* he thinks. *I'm not going to pay seventy-five dollars an hour to some professional because sex is as frequent as Haley's comet, and our relationship is as shallow as the spilled tea on my saucer,* she broods. While perhaps not legally divorcing, in an effort to avoid embarrassment or the admission that their intimacy has actually been a forgery, many couples emotionally divorce and become "married singles."

Couples aren't the only ones who assume premarital sex leaves no lasting consequences. Many of our trained counselors believe so as well. A well-respected and nationally-known Christian counselor told me in a casual conversation, "Premarital sex is nothing."

I stared at him, stunned. "Pardon?"

"It's nothing," he continued. "Now—rape, incest, adultery—those are the big [sins]. I deal with the big ones."

That he does. And his contribution to fixing the effects of the "big ones" is to be commended. Yet the "big ones" affect a small number of people, albeit in highly visible ways. Premarital sex affects a larger number of people but in less visible ways. Premarital sex produces communication difficulties, sexual hesitancies, lack of trust, and lack of respect. These less visible problems need to be dealt with in as serious a way as the effects of the "big ones."

It is interesting how we tend to minimize sin. The "big ones" and the "little ones" all carry disease. Cancer begins with a single cell. If I were to offer you a big cancer cell or a little cancer cell, would you take the little one? You'd take neither, because all cancer cells grow and destroy. So does all sin.

We all hope for a marriage that is cancer-free. We want the intimacy that we achieve to be healthy. But when we have engaged in premarital sex, we arrive at the altar under the shadow of impending disease. When we pursue legitimate needs through counterfeit means, we create impediments to achieving marital health through authentic intimacy. "What Satan has done," says Dr. Tony Evans, "has gotten you, like Eve, to focus on the tree you can't have. When you focus on the tree you can't have, you miss out on the one hundred trees you can have. Satan has you focusing on the sex you can't have, and you end up missing out on all of the *relationship* you can have!"[8]

As for me, I ended up missing out on the wedding little girls dream of. Our churches had already been reserved for the night we chose to get married, and we had to find another church in a hurry. That was no easy task in a small town, so we moved our search to the next town. The hormonal adjustment that came with my pregnancy made making the arrangements a chore. In our youth and immaturity, moments of confusion bred hateful words. So much difficulty aroused emotional instability.

Not knowing how to cope with the suddenness of everything, we would soon find ourselves dragging our feet toward the altar. In fact, I kicked mine the night before. Capitalizing on my vocal training as a cheerleader, I told Brian—and the neighbors—"I don't want to get married! No way. Not now. Things are going too fast." Throwing my ring at him, while throwing a fit, I crumbled under the reality that I was about to marry under protest. And Brian was about to marry out of panic rather than love.

What a way to start a family.

Section 2

The Challenges to Intimacy

3

Wounds of Love

"She's not going to wear white!" The tone was firm. A few days before our wedding, a group of people gathered to discuss arrangements, and the topic of dress color had come up.

"She's not wearing white," the individual said again. He was serious. My heart was in my throat. I needed to wear white. To, at least, wear white. I would have if I weren't pregnant. What had changed?

My pregnancy made me no guiltier than before, just more aware of my guilt. I, like many other nonvirgins, would have worn white if I weren't pregnant—simply out of tradition. The color of my gown did not reflect my purity. If it did then I, like everyone else, would need to wear black. No person on earth, barring Jesus, is really pure.

Yet, in our pharisaical attempts to legislate morality, we sometimes invent different gradations of purity and then award outward signs of honor to them. In doing so, we attempt to validate external appearances. We do this forgetting that, while people look at the outside, God sees our naked hearts. We do this forgetting that Jesus says, "Everyone who looks at a woman to lust for her has committed adultery with her already in his heart" (Matt. 5:28).

We do this forgetting that all have sinned, and no one really deserves to wear white.

Because all are sinners, the Lord has given us examples of how to show compassion when a life does not warrant the wearing of white, which is—this side of heaven—always. We see Jesus' example when, at a well, he speaks openly with a woman who has been married several times. We also see Him show mercy to a woman about to be stoned for prostitution. Yet another example comes through the life of a man named Joe.

Joseph was engaged to a teenaged girl named Mary. But there was one problem. Mary was pregnant. And since Joseph had never had relations with her, he came to the most logical conclusion: Mary had been unfaithful. As far as Joseph was concerned, Mary had sinned. And her sin was about to become very public. To marry her would be an admittance of guilt and participation—a grave thing in Jewish culture. Divorcing her in accordance with Jewish customs seemed like the only option. Within that option, there were two methods: public or private.

A public divorce would bring tremendous humiliation to Mary and her family—possibly even death by stoning for Mary. A private divorce before two witnesses, as the law also allowed, would accomplish the same end, yet without the humiliation. Joseph chose the latter, keeping both his conscience and compassion intact.

He did well. Surely pained, disappointed, and distraught, Joseph wanted to do the merciful thing. He didn't condone, but he didn't condemn. He loved Mary so much that he didn't want to disgrace her. "And Joseph her husband, being a righteous man, and not wanting to disgrace her, desired to put her away secretly" (Matt. 1:19). Mary had been blessed by God and had committed no sexual sin, but Joseph didn't know that. The angel had not yet met with Joseph to explain the situation. In fact, the manner of Jesus' conception wasn't revealed until after Joseph had decided what to do with Mary. But "Joseph, . . . being a righteous man," he simply sought to bring about the natural consequences in a compassionate manner. He responded in a righteous way.

First John 5:17 reads, "All unrighteousness is sin." *All.* But not all unrighteousness is visible. When a Christian girl is unmarried and pregnant, when she marries quickly and her stomach begins to expand too soon, her sin is exposed for the whole world to see. We sometimes look at her and think, "You have no right ever to wear white." We forget that all unrighteousness is sin, including our unrighteous judgment against her.

True, white is a symbol of purity, but true purity is solely a gift of grace. The saints who will return one day with our Lord will wear white but will do so, not by their own merit, but by His blood. Dare we say to the pregnant Christian teen that Christ's blood can atone for much but not this? Or, at least, not yet. Not until she has done time. Are we then not only seeking repentance but also punishment? Repentance leads to wholeness and vulnerability. Punishment brings only a bitter return. God handles consequences well enough on His own.

When we, as His people, add consequences outside the biblical direction for church discipline, one sin can turn into many. I know—when people judged me, I judged them back in self-defense. Thus, I compounded my sin by adding others, including pride and resentment.

We don't stone pregnant teenagers in the church today, at least not with physical objects. We do, however, sometimes stone them with our actions, our words, and our pointing fingers. Shortly after I got pregnant, I was used as an example to the congregation during a Sunday morning sermon—"This is what may happen if you disobey God." In a Sunday school class, a peer, glancing in my direction, said, "We need to remember that Jesus forgives *even* sexual sin. We should try and do the same."

Over the bridge between condoning and compassion walked a man named Joseph. He didn't know that Mary had done no wrong when he chose not to disgrace her. Neither did he choose to put her away in order to appear pious. His example is for our use. Yet when his example isn't followed, when people pass judgment—whether sinners against themselves or self-appointed moral guardians against sinners—it leaves those already vulnerable sinners even more vulnerable. In the case of Brian and me, the judgment of others undermined our marital intimacy and redirected our emotions.

Despite the opposition, I wore white. Yet, because of the opposition, I felt like an imposter. My self-condemnation further challenged intimacy. I had imagined that much of my appeal rested in my appearance. I questioned if Brian was even attracted to me anymore. I wondered if his loyalty was to me or to his own desires and ambitions. We both became defensive. And without premarital sex to distract us, our heightened uncertainties became our focus. Questioning increased our lack of trust. Lack of trust led to pointless arguments.

Just minutes after pledging to "love and to honor" each other at our wedding, we scuffled over who should have chosen our photographer. *Now, this is really important,* I thought. Yet I continued arguing. Through our smiles, we exchanged less than loving words as we posed for the wedding pictures.

After a casual honeymoon, Brian and I moved into the basement room where I lived. I hadn't remembered the room being so small. With the wedding over, the results of my futile quest for intimacy became public. Despite our best efforts to keep our quick wedding under wraps, most of the people in town had found us out even before the ceremony took place. My recent visit to the dentist hadn't helped the cover-up. A few days before the wedding, I had requested a lead apron while getting an X-ray. The dentist asked why, and in my naïveté I told him I was pregnant. By evening, I had received phone calls from friends wanting to find out about the news. Ah, life in a small town.

Although Brian and I had settled for counterfeit intimacy, we received well-meaning advice for establishing true marital intimacy. Our parents now became involved. Our pastors had their share to say. We were given books to read. Sometimes told what to do. Advice came from different sources, and most of it was contradictory. We were wished happiness and told not to blame each other by some. Others chided us for laughing and enjoying each other's company. One individual even told us that we had better stop laughing altogether.

Conflicting advice led to confusion, which became a steady companion. Confusion soon led to regret over our hasty decision to marry. I even called the Missouri State Court just five days after the wedding to see if I could get an annulment. The person on the phone said, "Sure, As long as you haven't consummated the marriage." I hung up.

There was no way out. The counterfeit intimacy we had so passionately created while dating now was suffocating beneath my confusion. I wanted out. Not out of the relationship with Brian or the development of our baby. Not out of the quest. But I wanted out of our confusion. I wanted us to stop hurting each other. Things were going too fast. Too many hurtful words had already been said. Pride was becoming a barrier to saying "I'm sorry" because pride had become my only form of protection.

My need for authentic intimacy only grew, however, as we pulled away from each other in the confusion. After a few months, we moved out of the basement and into an apartment, hoping that a change of scenery would spark a new beginning.

The only thing that grew, however, was a pile of bills. We had gone from being teenagers, whose every financial and material need had been met by parents, to being adults who could barely afford to put milk on our cereal. I immediately went to work full-time, putting my college education temporarily on hold. Brian worked a part-time job along with his full-time college studies and baseball games. Our quest for intimacy had mutated into a quest for survival.

We each wondered, *How could my spouse, whom I rarely see, be worth this stress and my abandoned dreams?* To our immature and selfish minds, the answer was, "He isn't"; "She isn't." Not in our present forms. Resentment brewed along with our pain and disillusionment. I was literally pointed at and whispered about in grocery stores and in church. I quickly found new stores and simply stopped going to church. Brian and I faced constant financial strain, confusion about our future, and lack of time for each other.

As well, we faced the pain of transferring our loyalty from our parents to each other. My parents had been the only caretakers I had ever known. And I didn't want to transfer my loyalty to Brian, not after the reality of what we had done began to sink in. Anything my parents said became gold, and I began to question almost everything that Brian said.

Brian's mother had a garden the size of Rhode Island, and Brian was used to the best of meals. I barely knew how to boil macaroni, and a grocery budget of twenty-five dollars a week limited the items on our grocery list.

Our new home was not very peaceful. Before we were married, I had circled the days on my calendar when we had sex. Now that we were married, I circled the days we didn't fight. In our first year of marriage, rarely did I circle more than one day a month. It didn't matter what we fought about, because what we were fighting about was never the real issue. Our embrace of counterfeit intimacy had left us emotionally empty yet saddled with a ton of responsibilities. We felt as if we had been deceived.

Each fight only reinforced how totally inadequate we were to meet each other's needs. Brian reminded me that most wives knew how to sort laundry so that white socks didn't turn pink. I reminded him that most husbands worked full-time, although I knew it was better in the long run that he finish college. Each fight only drove the wedge between us deeper, making intimacy seem as distant as a pot of gold at the end of the rainbow.

I longed for oneness and perfection in our relationship, and that was why I so resented Brian when I recognized his incompleteness. Having to pick up a dirty glass didn't just annoy me—it infuriated me. *I have not been raised to be a slave,* I thought. Without Jesus as the foundation for service, menial acts seemed demeaning.

With a typical teenage mentality, I thought it would be less irritating to pick up dirty glasses if I had a larger and better-decorated room, a bulging bank balance, and a kind husband. How much easier it would have been for a teenage Brian to take the dirty glass to the kitchen himself if he could expect the warm embrace of a petite partner instead of the weepiness of a partner who was pregnant and bombarded by hormones.

Awareness of one another's inadequacies often occurs when couples marry on the surface-level foundation of premarital sex, regardless of whether a pregnancy is involved or not. Brian and I faced problems that many other couples encounter—problems such as limited role development, inept interpersonal skills, and financial stress.

Limited Role Development

A 1956 home economics textbook reads,

> An hour before the husband is to arrive home from work, the wife is to bathe the children and place them in clean garments. The wife is to make sure that the girls' hair bows

and garments are neatly pressed. Then she is to prepare herself, applying fresh make-up and choosing an attractive outfit, for her husband's arrival home. When home, the wife and children should greet him outside. Inside, the wife should have dinner prepared. If dinner is unprepared, then the wife should sauté onions so at least the hint of dinner is in the air. After greeting the wife and children, the husband should be ushered to his bed to recline while the children return to their rooms. The wife should then take off his shoes and rub his feet until dinner is ready.

Roles have certainly changed. But God didn't create Adam and Eve Cleaver. He created Adam as head and Eve as helper—equal yet different in their roles. Roles signify neither hierarchy nor value. In the Trinity, God is one yet manifested through three distinct persons—Father, Son, and Holy Spirit. Jesus does the will of the Father while the Holy Spirit is referred to in Scripture as the Helper. Jesus, however, is not less than God, and the Holy Spirit is not less than either—they merely have different roles. For a woman to serve in the role of helper is not demeaning. Consider that the Holy Spirit holds the same title, and we worship Him with highest regard and honor.

When young adults marry, they often don't have a mature understanding of the way their roles within marriage should be fulfilled. Both husbands and wives have external as well as internal roles within the marriage. If a young man walks straight into marriage from his mother's home, he likely has not developed the skills or mind-set to be the provider for his family. This includes more than the external role of providing financial resources. It also includes the internal role of providing spiritual leadership, emotional stability, direction, and more. Instead, if a young man enters marriage still thinking that Mom or Dad is the provider, he may turn to his wife to fill that role rather than accept it himself. To accept it requires self-sacrifice, something he may not possess the spiritual maturity to practice.

The young woman may enter marriage having never done more around the house than earn her allowance by dusting and vacuuming. She may be clueless about providing meals and keeping a home as a way to esteem her husband. She may still equate domestic work with earning rewards rather than with service and an act of cultivating virtues. A young woman may also not understand a wife's internal role of providing for the best interests of others or submitting to her husband's leadership in a spirit of trust and joy.

A biblical view of roles in marriage doesn't come with age. A biblical view simply comes with grace, for it goes against our natural tendencies toward self. We are sinners, and we need to be taught, through God's grace, what He desires. A history of premarital sex had only reinforced internally our tendencies toward self.

Inept Interpersonal Skills

The key to any good marriage is communication. Building a strong relationship requires that we communicate when we are happy, sad, disappointed, excited, and all the other thoughts and feelings we might have. Two areas that can be adversely affected by a misdirected quest for intimacy are romantic communication and communication during conflict.

Romantic Communication

Romantic communication is essential in cultivating a healthy and vital marriage. During the dating stage, a great deal of energy is devoted to romance. But when a couple marries on a foundation that includes past partners or that is based on sex alone, the stresses and demands of a new marriage override romantic communication. And when children are added, the demands of parenting limit any remaining resources for cultivating it.

Communication During Conflict

Along with healthy, romantic communication, couples should learn to communicate properly during conflict. Every marriage will experience conflict. That's a given. How conflicts are handled and resolved affects the couple's intimacy and vulnerability. Hurtful words and actions create distance in relationships, which in turn causes more friction and resentment.

First, young adults often have inadequate skills for handling conflict. No one comes out of the womb ready and able to manage conflict perfectly. We are naturally selfish. Healthy conflict resolution grows out of an intense desire for God to transform our character. As this transformation takes priority over all other desires, we are able to consider other's needs above our own. Conflict management takes practice and a willingness to concede. People who have a history of selfishness—evident in premarital sex—aren't always known for their strengths in conceding.

Second, the thought patterns of young adults have not always matured enough to include abstract influences and ramifications. Many believe that the young adult mind functions in the formal operational mode—weighing the value of things in the present versus things to come.[1] While this may be true in some cases, it has also been demonstrated that young adults in our culture often act out of the concrete operational mode—having their thoughts gravitate toward immediate, concrete consequences and activities. Thoughts and emotions remain focused on immediate and visual stimuli, which results in reactionary thinking rather than proactive thinking.

When a young wife, for example, sees dirty dishes on the table

hours after her husband's breakfast, she may become angry. She sees
dirty dishes and immediately equates them with laziness and apathy
on her husband's part. He has plenty of energy, she notices, to wash
his car for the second time that week. She might even begin to feel
offended that her husband would expect her to clean up after him.
She does not see, however, that her own expectations clash with
those of her husband. Expectations come from a variety of sources—
family, peers, television. Nor does she recognize a pile of dirty dishes
as an opportunity to develop her own spiritual maturity by cultivating the virtues of service and grace. Rather, she may choose to leave
the dishes on the table, giving her husband a reason to be frustrated
over her lack of cleaning skills. He may later erupt in anger, or in the
end she may clear the table, all the while grumbling and saving up
his offense for ammunition later.

Couples with counterfeit marital intimacy may also be quicker
to hit below the belt. Hitting below the belt includes anything
emotionally and psychologically hurtful to the other person. Name-
calling, using demeaning words, speaking with the intent to hurt,
disrespecting the other person's family, threatening divorce, swearing, or bringing up the other person's weaknesses or failures are all
examples of hitting below the belt. Spiteful words force the taking
of sides.

A lack of healthy communication during conflicts can kill affection and intimacy in a marriage by removing the safe environment needed for honesty and vulnerability.

Financial Stress

In most marriages, regardless of their foundation, financial mat-
ters rate high on the list of stressors. But in a relationship that is
already distrusting because of premarital sex, financial issues are
amplified.

Often young newlyweds have not dealt with budgets before, nor are they used to living on limited resources. Their standards of living may take a nose-dive when they move out of their parents' homes or leave single lifestyles to get married.

Leaving home should mean becoming financially self-sufficient. That, however, is rarely the case for two young people who are finishing high school or college or who have just embarked on new careers. Parents may be tempted to help with finances. Yet care needs to be taken to allow the new relationship to thrive financially on its own. The young husband needs to be nurtured in his new responsibilities as provider more than he needs to be bailed out. If parents, in-laws, or friends usurp this role, the husband is not only prevented from meeting his responsibilities, but the young wife may find it more difficult to transfer her respect to the new head of her home.

The solution to the financial-aid dilemma lies in the creativity of those helping. Money needs to come, not as a handout but as a gift, at appropriate times such as Christmas, birthdays, or anniversaries. Even better, it can be earned. Providing evening or weekend odd jobs is a great way to help couples in financial difficulties without creating a physical or emotional dependency on the ones offering the help.

Couples should also be aware that limited resources in a materialistic society could be a source of tension in their marriage. The media and peers constantly bombard the new couple with images of things that are touted as necessary for comfort and happiness. When the young couple realizes that their own resources barely provide a one-bedroom apartment, food, and fuel, they may feel as if they are failing. They may forget that most of the people they're comparing themselves with also began with paltry means.

When, in the first stages of our marriage, Brian and I were struggling financially, Brian inwardly compared his nineteen-year-old's beginning hourly wage with my father's established salary. Little wonder he questioned his role as provider. At the time, he didn't see the comparison was unfair.

For some young married couples, financial difficulties may be exacerbated as a result of premarital sex. If a young man fathers a child out of wedlock, he must support that child financially. Sexually transmitted diseases (STDs) require visits to the doctor. And STDs frequently cause infertility. If a young person suffering from an STD marries and wants children, it can lead to huge expenditures for fertility treatments and surgeries.

Many young adults faced with financial pressures don't realize, as I didn't at the time, that happiness doesn't come with what you have but with how you perceive what you have. The ultimate solution to financial stress comes only through placing your trust in God as your provider and source of contentment. In the Bible, Paul had learned to be content with much or little. Young couples in new marriages have the opportunity to grow spiritually by developing the virtue of contentment.

Ultimately the answers to these dilemmas of role development, communication, and financial stress lie in the spiritual maturity of each person. The quest for marital intimacy must be accompanied by a quest for spiritual growth, or it will inevitably falter.

I know. Shortly before the birth of our daughter, one of our fights escalated. When it was over, our marriage certificate lay torn in shreds on the floor among the remains of rose petals and chicken noodle soup. I had done the tearing as well as the tossing of the soup. Later, Brian painstakingly found all the pieces of our certificate and taped it up.

And while tape works well on paper, it would require more than that to mend our hearts.

4

First Comes Love.
Then Comes Baby.
Then Comes Marriage
in a Baby Carriage.

While not every couple that engages in premarital sex ends up pregnant or even married, some, of course, do. These couples face unique challenges to marital intimacy. Not every couple will have the same experience as Brian and I, but for those who have been in similar straits, this chapter discusses the effects of an early pregnancy and premature marriage.

In some ways, a premature marriage may be compared to a premature birth. Rather than enjoying months of sweet anticipation and preparation, the mother of a premature baby is dashed to the hospital with very little notice. The fragile and underdeveloped newborn arrives with a variety of medical problems. Similarly, Brian and I, rather than enjoying an extended period of engagement, rushed prematurely to the chapel. After we were married, the natural results of our underdeveloped relationship manifested themselves— lack of romance, mutual blame, and distrust. It was obvious to us that our relationship was weakening, but because I was afraid everyone would find out what I had done, I was ashamed to admit any more weaknesses. Pride became my security blanket. The condition of our relationship deteriorated further, then, as I refused to consider treatment. Months after our wedding, the weakened condition of our premature marriage set off alarms that indicated heart failure.

We had no forewarning of all this. I was confused and in shock. The popular marriage books I had been given to read were so far beyond my level of maturity and so far removed from my anger that they seemed surreal. They contained information on subjects such as ways to improve your relationship through bonding exercises or "date-nights." While I struggled with adjustments, resentment, and confusion, I read about a "date-night." *How sweet,* I thought.

There's not much helpful information being published from a Christian perspective for couples in premature marriages. And beyond that, the evangelical population has largely ignored the whole topic of premarital sex. Thus, many of us are left high and dry with little Christian support and advice when deciding whether or not to marry following sexual intimacy and the resulting pregnancy.

Young adults who are adjusting to parenthood and marriage experience a huge level of stress. It's not an easy road. Perhaps that is why, out of all the options available to pregnant teens—adoption, abortion, single parenthood, and marriage—marriage is the least likely to be chosen. *People* magazine recently ran a cover story on twenty-five teen parents.[1] *None* of the teenagers the magazine tracked over a five-year period married the other parent of their first baby. None. When marriage, however, is chosen, it carries an extremely high rate of divorce—60 percent within the first six years.[2] Knowing this, I can only give glory to God for His grace in bringing us to where we are as a family today.

Young families often fall apart early due to the high stress levels that occur during periods of multiple transitions. From college psychology, Brian discovered that stress levels rise during transitions. We learned that information a little late. He also learned that stress levels increase the most during such major transitions as moving, getting married, becoming pregnant with a first child, starting a new job, giving birth, or a death in the family. Singly, each transition can usually be handled well, and the "crisis stage"— the length of time at crisis level—held to a short period. Yet when multiple changes occur simultaneously, the potential increases for an extended crisis stage.

In the four weeks surrounding our wedding, Brian and I experienced three of these major transitions. We were about to experience three more over the next eight months. Within the first year of our marriage, we faced *six* of these major transitions that produce high stress levels. We also experienced an accident that totaled our only car and could have resulted in serious injury had God not protected me and the baby in my womb.

From the onset of our marriage, Brian and I had experienced an exaggerated level of crisis due to multiple simultaneous transitions: marriage, moving, first pregnancy, body changes, new job for Brian, new job for me, moving again, quitting college to go to work, changing to another new job so I could go back to college, changing colleges altogether, financial stress, and the impending birth of our new baby. Needless to say, our emotions were unstable.

When it came time for our baby to be born, I was already on overload, both mentally and emotionally. Following twelve hours of labor I rested for an hour, then the nurse brought my baby to me. She placed all eight pounds and four ounces of this tiny new life in my arms. After the nurse left—which was way too quickly— I became afraid. There we were, my baby and I alone in a silent room. My mind flooded with questions.

Feeding-time presented my first challenge—that of rolling over. The pain from the delivery still racked my body. On top of that, I had to navigate the roll now while holding a delicate and breakable infant.

Doesn't the nurse know I'm just a teenager? I thought. *Doesn't she know about my guinea pigs and fish?* Most of them died under my care. *How could she just hand me my baby and walk away?* I had never even baby-sat an infant before. I couldn't remember ever holding one.

The fear of accidentally dropping my newborn paralyzed me. Several minutes passed before I summoned the courage to roll over. And in that moment I realized that eight pounds and four ounces is really a ton—a ton of responsibility, change, and challenge.

"You go from no responsibility to tremendous responsibility with no baby steps," writes Faith, now married with four children—whose first child came at age fifteen. "It is so easy to expect that someone else will help because it wasn't too long ago when someone was doing everything for you."

The nurse had followed proper procedure in leaving my baby alone with me. I, after all, was her mother. Yet my teenage mind wondered why the nurse hadn't stayed to take care of things. I wondered why she didn't ask, "Is there anything I can do? Would you like me to nurse her for you?" I was used to my mom making my lunches, washing my clothes, and helping me with my room. A shift in thinking doesn't occur in the time it takes for a baby to exit the birth canal.

A teenager's mind functions differently from that of a mature adult. Researchers, using modern medical technology, measured brain-wave activity and discovered there are major variances between the locations of brain activity in adults versus teens.[3] Their studies showed that teenagers often use a different portion of their brain than adults do.

As we have already noted, a number of young adults still use reactionary thought processes rather than proactive ones. Reactionary thinking gravitates toward immediate, concrete consequences and activities. When the nurse handed me my daughter, for example, my mind focused on how I was going to roll over without dropping her. I didn't think what her temperament, personality, gifts, or talents might be. I didn't consider how I would raise her, discipline her, or pay for her school activities and college. I just wanted to roll over without dropping her. After that was accomplished, I was able to think about the next thing—feeding her. Then the next—calling the nurse to come put her back in her baby bed.

Compare those thoughts to those I had six years later when another nurse handed me my newborn son. On that day, I wondered what plans God had for him, what experiences he would have, and how I would train him up to be a gentleman. The members of my Sunday school class had offered to prepare and deliver meals following his birth. I asked if they would, instead, spend the time praying for our son, and for Brian and me as his parents. By that time I was an adult, using a formal operational mode of thinking. I weighed the value of things in the present versus things to come. Of course, I still considered how to roll over without dropping him, but that thought alone didn't consume me.

Functioning within the concrete operational mode, as many young adults do, produces a reactionary form of parenting and relating. For example if a baby cries, she is consoled. If a baby spits up, she is cleaned. If a baby grows, she is bought new clothes. If she is hungry, she is fed. None of these things are wrong; in fact they are significant parts of parenting. Reactionary parenting alone, however, is not enough to nurture the healthy spiritual and emotional development of the child.

And reactionary relating is not enough to nurture marital intimacy either. With each new transition, Brian and I merely coped with, rather than solved, our difficulties. Each new transition sapped our mental energy. With the birth of our daughter, we poured the bulk of our mental and emotional resources into the legitimate and immediate needs of an infant. Little was left over for adjusting to the strains of teen parenthood—the distancing of extended family, internal conflicts, and peer tension.

Distancing of Extended Family

Even within a Christian home, an unplanned pregnancy will bring stress on family members. While Christianity may mature families and enable them to respond better as support systems in times of crises, it hasn't always promoted honest communication when conflicts need to be resolved. Parents, grandparents, or siblings may not wish to add to the stress of the new young mother's situation with their own hurts or disappointments. Oftentimes, in an effort to support her through the crisis, immediate and extended family members may suppress feelings of anger, disappointment, and shame. Over time, these pent-up emotions can create distance in relationships, causing strained family dynamics.

If family relationships function poorly prior to the pregnancy, the pregnancy may only increase alienation. If the teenager has not experienced acceptance or approval before becoming pregnant, the public shame of an unwed pregnancy will oftentimes intensify disapproval.

Distance develops, too, during the transition into new roles. My parents and I were forced to undergo a quick change in responsibilities without much preparation. In a four-week period, I went from having a child-parent relationship with my folks to an adult-adult relationship. My immaturity didn't, of course, always reflect my new role as an adult, but my parents tried to treat me as one in order to help me.

Distance can also develop as a young girl tries to figure out how much she wants her parents to be involved in her new life. Too much involvement hinders the teenager's personal growth and maturity. Too little involvement gives rise to decisions that lack depth and wisdom and that may lead to improper parenting of the new child and less-than-honoring decisions as a wife. This time of transition is a tightrope, and even the smallest of slips produces bruising.

Internal Conflicts

As a pregnant teenager, I struggled to find balance between what I perceived as my needs and the legitimate needs of my child. These struggles were mired in loss of opportunity, loss of belonging, and loss of identity.

Loss of Opportunity

Being a cheerleader and pom-pom girl in high school was fun. I had led thousands of people in cheers at local sporting events. I valued those times in my teen years, but when it came time for me to try out for pom-pom in college, I had a newborn. Because I was a teen, I had shrunk back to my pre-pregnancy size after only a few weeks, but my size and ability were no longer the only considerations. I now had to consider my availability and priorities.

Would pom-pom be fun? Yes. Was there anything wrong with it? No. Those used to be my only considerations. Now I had three new questions. Would my family benefit? Would my family suffer from my time commitment? Who would watch my child? My mom had already accepted a full schedule of baby-sitting while I worked and went back to college part-time.

Job training, education, and work may be necessary for a teen parent. Cheerleading, parties, and extracurricular activities are not. But to me—functioning in the immediacy of concrete operational thinking—those things seemed necessary. When I couldn't do them, I experienced internal conflict. I valued my little girl and wanted her to be well, but I missed the fun of just being a teen in college. I didn't know how to do both.

Loss of Belonging

Beyond the obvious changes in activities for a teenage parent are the subtle reminders of what has occurred. Sylvia, a teen counselor, states that "while teens may regain their slender form, enabling them to don the latest pair of hip-huggers, stretch marks serve as a constant reminder that their hip-huggers don't look like everyone else's." Hip-huggers weren't around yet when I had my daughter, but I had to toss out my two-piece swimsuit and buy a new one that would cover my stretch marks. I don't give a second thought to having stretch marks today, but when I was a teenager they were a constant reminder that I was different.

The felt need to belong ranks almost as high, for most teens, as the need for food and shelter. Selfish needs often distort the decision-making process, becoming more important than the developmental needs of the child. The tension between what the child needs and what the teen parent perceives as her own needs gives rise to internal conflict, even though the teenager, at least at some level, recognizes the dependent nature of her child.

In my college classes, I was known as the girl who looked way too young to have a baby. "You have a baby?" people would frequently ask. I was frighteningly skinny after the birth of our first-born and that added fuel to their conversations. Another girl in college became pregnant and had her baby when I was a sophomore. Rather than sympathizing with her struggles, I remember feeling happy, because now I would have someone with whom I could relate. Sad, I know.

Loss of Identity

A loss of identity can also occur as the teenager struggles to determine which world she lives in—the world of a parent or the world of a teen. The reality that she actually lives in neither, but in the new world of the teen-parent, is sometimes tough to swallow. Feeling rejection from peers, many teens may just opt for the role of parent. "I think to be able to make it you have to be able to let everything you want go for a time," writes Melody, who became a mother while still in high school. "That is hard when the teen years are the time in people's lives when they are beginning to see who they are and what they want to do. There is a sense of identity that gets bypassed when you are a teen mother."

Peer Tension

Finally, another adjustment a teenage parent experiences relates to tension within her peer group.

"You get old before you are old," recounts Shawna of her time in high school as a teen mother. "Even still, ten years later, talking to people my age is very difficult because most of them don't even have kids yet. When I went back to school after having Chase, I hated it so much. I almost didn't graduate just because I hated being there. I thought the other kids acted so immature—almost to the point of making me sick! Their big concern was where the next party was and what shoes they would wear for school the next day. It was hard to listen to that when I had been up all night with a screaming, colicky baby with a fever. For me to get ready for school meant I had to get dressed as well as dress the baby, pack diapers, make bottles, and walk out the door with all my school-work. I sat in class and thought about the responsibilities I had to meet before I could even do my homework that night."

For teen parents to maintain social relationships within previous peer groups requires grace, patience, and understanding from all parties. Teenagers generally do not possess the maturity to carry it off.

While friends may intend to stay close during the pregnancy, the actual birth of the baby creates a significant gap in priorities and interests. Teen moms and their friends naturally drift apart. The teen parent then often experiences isolation from peers during the transitional years after high school or even college.

Peer isolation can carry, too, into adulthood. Adult relationships in churches and communities often form around the ages of the families' children. Brian and I generally found ourselves frustrated attending the young-married's Sunday school classes. We had little or nothing in common with childless newlyweds, even though we were the same age. But when we participated in classes for older couples who had been married a number of years and whose children were the same ages as ours, we found ourselves with people at least ten and sometimes twenty years older. Because of the current trend to delay marriage and families, the social gap between today's teenage parents and parents who have children of the same age is often huge. Differences in interests and maturity levels may thus distance teenage parents from a variety of peer groups.

In only a short time, I had gone from having a substantial peer group to having no one. I tried becoming friends with women who had children the same age as mine, but I was always lacking when it came to conversation, priorities, and values of care. They, for instance, could afford the latest in household goods and children's products for picnics or trips to the park. Their cheese, grapes, and lunch meat were cut into perfect pieces for tiny hands. They sang all the finger plays and nursery rhymes. I sat there looking at their perfectly packed provisions and then to the peanut butter and jam sandwich, potato chips, and coke tossed in my bag—albeit my child had the best in designer baby clothes, even if that meant spending less on groceries. As you might imagine, my friends and I didn't understand each other very well. Nor did we remain friends for long.

I tried spending time with a friend from high school only to be bored by her incessant talk about who got drunk at what party. Or who quit her job at the town café. Or who planned to go "mudding" that weekend. Please.

It was easier to give up altogether on finding friends. Ironically, my quest for authentic intimacy, which had taken a wrong turn with premarital sex, had left me even more lonely.

5

Not as Strong
as We Think

A little over a year into our marriage, Brian and I purchased a very small, one-bedroom house. Again, we thought a change of scenery might improve our perspectives. It didn't.

A month after we moved in, I moved out. Our fighting, which had occurred regularly since the wedding, had become more in tense. Our words now seethed with hate. In two years of dating, we had argued only once. Brian had been angry with me only that one time, and then very briefly and very controlled. And I had been angry with him only that one time as well.

Now we targeted our disappointments at one another. I was disappointed that I had to work besides taking on the responsibilities at home and limiting my extracurricular college activities. Brian was disappointed that our marriage had created friction within his family. I was disappointed that boys on campus treated me better than my own husband did. Brian was disappointed that girls on campus treated him better than his own wife did. I was disappointed that I was lonely. We were both disappointed that we couldn't ever get along.

It wasn't the disappointment, though, that caused me to leave. It is what we did with our disappointment. We tried to crucify each other with our words—daily. After so many months of dishing it out and receiving it, I no longer cared about hope. I no longer cared about God's judgment if we divorced. I no longer cared about forgiving or seeking forgiveness.

So I filed for a divorce. Although Brian said he didn't want a divorce, he signed the papers giving me no contest. He said he knew I was serious, and he wanted to cooperate in order to avoid further nastiness. *Great,* I thought. *So the divorce is all of a sudden on my shoulders.*

The court date was set for a few months later. The announcement ran in the local paper—more grist for the small-town gossip mill. Our marriage was on the ropes. The challenges to creating and developing marital intimacy had annihilated it.

Anyone who has engaged in premarital sex will face challenges later in regard to marital intimacy. Recognizing and acknowledging the challenges are the first steps to overcoming them. Engaging in premarital sex creates a hindrance to healthy marital sex, may cause health problems, increases the risk of infidelity, and intensifies family difficulties.

A Hindrance to Healthy Marital Sex

Premarital sex often devastates marital sex. Only within an intimate and trusting relationship can sexual partners be vulnerable and experience mutual satisfaction. Yet premarital sex often gives rise to doubts about one another's integrity. For the first two years of our marriage, I assumed that the punishment for our premarital sex was awful sex for the rest of my life. I didn't realize that our marriage bed was simply tainted with anger. "The reason why people don't have good sex is simply because they don't like each other," says marriage counselor Dr. Willard Harley.[1] "It's difficult to be intimate with someone you can't stand."

Lisa, a woman who had engaged in premarital sex said, "It took us nearly ten years to rework how we thought about sex so that we could enjoy it." This is because premarital sex produces an inaccurate model by which to gauge arousal. It fosters a self-pleasing spirit. It also produces guilt feelings that become associated with the very act of sex.

"Nathan and I have been married almost ten years," wrote Stacie, a woman who had engaged in premarital sex, "and it was only last summer that I finally realized that making love to my husband was something that actually brought God joy. Talk about a revelation. I had even got to the point that I would not make love to my husband on Sundays because I really felt like it was a 'dirty' thing. My whole idea of sex, the way God really designed it, had been altered because of what was done prior to this union."

When we have trained ourselves to focus on our personal pleasure as the primary goal in sex, a necessary element for marital intimacy has been discarded. That necessary element is honor. As Christ loved us, so He has asked us to love each other. He has instructed us to do so with honor by being harmonious, sympathetic, brotherly, kindhearted, and humble in spirit.

Being *harmonious* means pursuing the same goals. *Sympathetic* means being responsive to the other person's needs. *Brotherly* means living with your mate as a companion. *Kindhearted* means having affection and being sensitive to things that annoy the other person. Being *humble in spirit* means being selfless. Healthy marital sex, then, is the culmination of a relationship that is rooted in biblical love.

Premarital sex is the pursuit of personal satisfaction—be it acceptance, pleasure, or security—at the expense of someone else's honor. Seth, now a respected Christian leader who had engaged in premarital sex as a teenager, tells how he had to change his mind about sex after he got married. "Not only did I have to repent of my sin of premarital sex," he said, "but I also had to reevaluate what I thought to be the purpose of sexual relations and then align my view with God's view. It took many years into our marriage for me to reprogram my thinking and become able to give myself to my wife as God had intended."

Premarital sex may also train us to manipulate circumstances in our marriage to obtain sexual pleasure. Healthy marital sex delights itself in satisfying one another's desires, even when one partner's desire is not aroused. Yet premarital sex fosters a mindset that sex is all about *me*. When we don't get what that "me" wants, we become angry. The object of our love turns into the object of our contempt precisely because he or she was only that—an object, not a person made in the image of God.

Consider King David's son Amnon who desired his beautiful half-sister, Tamar, so fiercely that he became physically sick with love (see 2 Sam. 13:1–2). After he eventually cornered her through a ruse and raped her, his feverish love turned into an intense hate. Just before the rape, Tamar begged Amnon to ask their father David to let Amnon marry her so as not to dishonor her. Yet Amnon wanted what he wanted, and he wanted it right then. After he got it, though, Amnon "hated her with a very great hatred; for the hatred with which he hated her was greater than the love with which he had loved her. And Amnon said to her, 'Get up, go away!'" (v. 15).

Getting what we want through manipulation brings disdain, dishonor, and guilt. Future marital relations are hindered, even though they are meant to be pure.

Physical Pain and Limitations

Premarital sex may also breed sexually transmitted diseases. The author of Proverbs warns about sex outside of marriage, "And you groan at your latter end, when your flesh and your body are consumed" (Prov. 5:11).

HIV, chlamydia, ghonerea, herpes, hepatitis, genital warts, and syphilis are among some of the diseases that plague those who indulge in unmarried sex. Not only do these diseases bring pain but, in many cases, they also bring serious consequences. Many women with STDs will never be able to conceive a child. "I was so upset," writes one girl about the STD she contracted at age sixteen, "I couldn't leave the doctor's office. . . . I was amazed to learn that most STDs, including the one I had, don't have many symptoms, especially in women. . . . The only way to detect most STDs is with an examination. Left untreated, the infection I had can cause infertility."[2]

The physical consequences of premarital sex may last a lifetime or cut a lifetime short. "Ninety percent of cervical cancer cases are believed to be associated with HPV [human papilloma virus] infections," reports one medical journal. "Sexually transmitted hepatitis B is an important contributing factor to liver cancer and ectopic pregnancy, which is the leading cause of maternal mortality. Trichomoniasis has been linked with an increased risk of pelvic inflammatory disease and preterm labor, which is associated with low birth weight and premature birth. Ulcerative and discharging diseases, such as herpes, trichomoniasis and syphilis, have been linked to an increased risk of both becoming infected with and transmitting HIV."[3]

Trisha, a woman physically scarred by premarital sex, writes,

> Free love. Free sex. I learned there is nothing free about it. My husband and I are paying a tremendous price for the lifestyle I chose before I married! . . . At my premarital checkup, I was surprised when my Pap smear came back abnormal, indicating precancerous cells. This was the result of a

sexually transmitted disease called the Human Papilloma
Virus (HPV). I also learned my husband and I would need
to abstain from sexual relations for up to eight weeks while
I received treatment. This was not an exciting way to begin a marriage!

The eight weeks of abstinence turned into seven long
months as we underwent various treatments. I endured
cryo-surgery three times. . . . All the surgeries had damaged my cervix making it impossible for sperm to enter
my uterus and fallopian tubes. . . . Every month we went
to the physician's office so he could inject my husband's
sperm into my vagina and bypass the damaged portion of
my cervix. . . . After four surgeries, fourteen unsuccessful
inseminations and thousands of dollars, my husband and
I have given up hope of having a child. I clearly recognize
the tremendous price we have paid for the lifestyle I chose
before I married.[4]

When we exchange glorifying God for glorifying mankind, God
often permits us to suffer the consequences of our own unwise
behavior. "*For this reason* God gave them over to degrading pas-
sions . . . and [they received] in their own persons the due penalty
of their error" (Rom. 1:26–27, emphasis added).

Risk of Infidelity

Premarital sex often lays the groundwork for infidelity. Much
of the enticement of premarital sex lies, after all, in the lure of the
forbidden. "But sin, taking opportunity through the commandment, produced in me coveting of every kind" (Rom. 7:8). We
often want unmarried sex simply because we are not supposed to
have it. Our sinful selves delight in deeds of rebellion. When we

have participated in premarital sex, we have trained our bodies to enjoy illicit excitement. We have literally trained our bodies in greed.

Brian and I have a joke we use to chide each other with whenever we experience an inconvenience. If we have to sit too long at a stoplight, stand too long in a checkout line, or if the video we want to rent has already been checked out, we turn to each other and say, tongue-in-cheek, "This shouldn't happen. We're in America!"

We say it as a gentle reminder that most people don't have the conveniences that Americans do. We say it to remind ourselves of the silliness of our own impatience. We become irritated at the prolonged stoplight only because we have become accustomed to not having to wait.

Likewise, couples may become bored with marital relations if they have become accustomed to illicit sex. When sex is no longer illicit, it may not be very tempting. Some married couples find that the sexual fireworks they experienced before marriage turn into duds following the wedding. Their bodies have become accustomed to feeding upon a forbidden smorgasbord. Marriage turns the smorgasbord into a TV dinner.

When boredom occurs, we may turn elsewhere for pleasure. *Elsewhere* includes adultery, masturbation, pornography, books, or even romantic dramas and soap operas. Infidelity does not always mean having a physical affair. Many people carry on affairs with their jobs, ministries, books, emotional attachments to coworkers, or hobbies.

Family Difficulties

Premarital sex can lay the groundwork for family difficulties later. It can turn the couple into a poor role model for their children. It can increase arguments. It can cause the couple to rely on sex to validate their relationship or solve conflicts.

A Poor Role Model for Children

Engaging in premarital sex may affect the emotional well-being of children who are born into the marriage. When God decreed His Ten Commandments, He began by addressing idolatry: "You shall have no other gods before Me. You shall not make for yourself an idol . . . for I, the LORD your God, am a jealous God" (Exod. 20:3–5).

When I elevated Brian and myself higher than God by violating His command against premarital sex, I committed spiritual idolatry. Spiritual idolatry occurs when we elevate things other than God so that they become "objects of extreme devotion."[5] God's jealous response to this idolatry spans across generations as the verse in the commandment continues: ". . . visiting the iniquity of the fathers on the children, on the third and the fourth generations" (v. 5).

For premarital sex to render the couple a poor role model for their children requires no more than the natural outgrowth of the sin. Whether or not the children ever know about what the couple did before they got married, they will be asked to live under a relationship rooted in sin. Sin changes behaviors.

It has been said that the greatest gift a father can give his child is to love his wife. When premarital sex is the foundation of a couple's unity, the relationship is rooted in dishonor. Even if premarital sex is not recognized as dishonor, it will reveal itself in the way the couple relate to one another. If a woman was not cherished or the man was not respected prior to the marriage—evident in premarital sex—he or she can expect to receive the same lack of honor when married. That is, until the root of their sin is dealt with.

Honoring a person means considering the well-being of that person to be more important than your own. Premarital sex is the opposite of honor. Even if a woman thinks, at the time, that she is something special to her man, in order to restore true honor to the relationship she must acknowledge the truth of what she has done. She has contributed to his downfall by feeding his flesh and has helped to create or maintain a vice that will wedge its way between him and God.

Lack of honor prior to marriage will mean lack of honor after marriage, unless the sin is addressed. Lack of honor between parents is an inaccurate picture of love for children. As the children grow older, they will have to piece together their own image of intimacy using their parents' picture, which has been smeared, torn, or even lost altogether.

An Increase in Arguments

A couple with a history of premarital sex has established their union on a foundation of sand—that of hedonism. *Hedonism* means the pursuit of personal pleasure. When personal pleasure is the root of intimacy, everything springing up from that root will be tainted with deficiency. What we do on the surface may give the illusion of love, but the deep, heartfelt motivation remains personal pleasure, fulfillment, or gain. Such selfishness will undoubtedly lead to an increase in arguments, because the relationship lacks someone who will, in humility, yield without resentment.

The apostle James addressed selfishness when he wrote, "What is the source of quarrels and conflicts among you? Is not the source your *pleasures* that wage war in your members?" (James 4:1, emphasis added).

The Greek word from which we translate "pleasures" in this verse is *hedoni,* the same root word from which we derive *hedonism.*

In the verse above, James asks the Jewish Christians of his day, "Why are you fighting? What is causing your arguments and your distance? Isn't the cause of your fighting your own selfish pleasures?"

When I chose to engage in premarital sex, I gave myself a more accurate picture of who I really was. I had convinced myself that I was a polite and well-mannered person. My perception rested more, however, on what I thought I should be rather than on what I actually was. Like Alice in her imaginary wonderland, I had become a pawn to my own desires. I can sympathize with her regrets— *"While I often gave myself good advice, I very rarely followed it."*

My actions actually revealed a person with little self-control, personal discipline, or respect—both for others and myself. I was driven by my own pleasure and the desire to avoid responsibility. Should I have expected my character to change simply because I had gotten married? Rather, my character only revealed itself more under the weight of new stress.

After marriage, I felt helpless against my newfound limitations. These limitations made me angry, although I never *said* that they made me angry. I didn't even consciously *think* that they made me angry. Instead I directed my anger elsewhere. When Brian and I argued, I didn't really care about the things we argued over, although I'm sure it appeared that way. In actuality, the root of our conflicts was that my pleasures had been threatened. Recall what James said concerning arguments: "Is not the source [of quarrels] your *pleasures* . . . ?" (emphasis added).

A couple's lack of love for one another is not because of hatred but because of selfishness. "Hate is not the opposite of love," says youth speaker Dawson McAllister. "Selfishness is the opposite of love."[6] And as we've seen in the book of James, selfish pleasure, *hedoni,* breeds quarrels.

A Reliance on Sex to Validate the Relationship or Solve Conflict

Webster defines *intimate* as "belonging to or characterizing one's deepest nature; marked by a warm friendship developing through long association."[7] Conflict arising from a foundation of premarital sex destroys friendship and has the potential to limit the length of any relationship. Premarital sex harms a relationship during the dating stage because couples adopt a pattern of easing tension and measuring compatibility through sexual activity. Thus, those who have a history of premarital sex often resort to sex to solve conflicts. They gauge the success of their marriage on how many times they've had sex in the last week and on its level of intensity and creativity.

"The first key about sex is patience," says Pastor Tommy Nelson.

> Whenever you are impatient in sex, you're going to do one of two things: you're going to harm a good relationship, or you're going to prolong a bad one. When I say harm a good relationship, one of the worst things you can do is to get into premarital sex because it teaches you to communicate on a surface level. Sex becomes the power of your marriage instead of [being] the follow-through. . . . You can't run a marriage on sex.[8]

A toddler, after scraping her knee, went to put some medicine on it as she had seen her mother do. Not knowing where the medicine was, she grabbed something that looked like it. It was in a tube like the one she'd seen her mother use. But the tube she grabbed was Super Glue. After pressing the Band-Aid down tightly, her "owie" felt better—for a time. Until her mother removed the bandage!

If sex is used to resolve conflicts before marriage, it will be used in the same way after marriage, like the toddler using Super Glue—in a mistaken attempt to heal wounds. On the surface it appears to be medicine, but it actually causes more harm than good. Things might "stick" together for a time, but the wounds don't heal any more than did the toddler's scrape. In fact, using sex to heal conflicts only makes the wounds worse.

If a couple doesn't change their view on premarital sex once they are married, they will continue to use sex as a substitute for real healing, thinking it's holding the marriage together. They will look to their marriage bed to tell them if they are close or not. Their intimacy will be no greater than their last sexual experience—and will last about as long.

Biblical love, however, is modeled after Jesus. It does not seek its own pleasure. "Biblical love is the decision to do what's best for the other person even if I have to get nailed to do it," says Dr. Tony Evans. "Biblical love is going to a cross in anticipation of a resurrection."[9] Note that the person who is resurrected is the same person who went to the cross. Biblical loving doesn't guarantee that a relationship will be revived. It only provides the opportunity. But "going to the cross" may mean that you find new life and complete intimacy from a heavenly source.

When we have created our own problems through sin, we commonly try to solve our own problems as well. But trying to solve our own problems through counselors, antidepressants, books, and a variety of other methods may encourage us to lose sight of God's solution. What the world often considers wisdom does not point people to God. On the contrary, it teaches them a list of proper behaviors and totally negates God's work in the soul.

Couples may leave the counselor's office with a list of things to do, but they lack the love and trust necessary to do them. "Couples who end up in my office have often already seen four, or five, or even six other counselors," said author and family counselor Roger Hillerstrom. "But those counselors had only dealt with changing the couple's behavior, rather than working through their history of premarital sex."[10]

When we have carried the mind-set of premarital sex into our marriage—the mind-set of self-seeking pleasure—we don't live in the way God says it's necessary to live in order to produce authentic intimacy birthed in true love. In fact, we embrace the opposite way. God says that love is love only when one is willing to lay down one's life for a friend. Laying down one's life means giving up everything for the benefit of another.

There's a humorous story about Adam in the Garden of Eden. Adam felt very lonely, and God asked him, "What is wrong with you?" Adam said he didn't have anyone to talk to. God said that he was going to make Adam a companion and that it would be a woman.

"This person," said God, "will gather food for you and cook for you. When you discover clothing, she'll wash it for you. She will always agree with every decision you make. She will bear your children and never ask you to get up in the middle of the night to take care of them. She won't nag you and will always be the first to admit she was wrong when you've had a disagreement. She'll never have a headache and will freely give you love and passion whenever you need it."

Adam asked God, "What will a woman like this cost?"

God replied, "An arm and a leg."

Adam thought for a moment and then asked, "What can I get for a rib?"

In this story, Adam gets less from a woman, because he isn't willing to give up more of himself. Sincere love does not come wrapped in self-interest but in sacrifice—laying down our lives. When our arms or legs are of more concern to us than God's plan for the lives of other people, especially our spouses, we will end up short on intimacy. A couple may live together, even have sex together, but that makes them no more intimate than moving to France makes me French.

The only way I will be allowed French citizenship is to commit myself to France—studying its laws and constitution. I must live there in a participatory manner for a number of years, work there, and finally apply for citizenship. If any of these things is not done, I'm still just an American living in France.

Likewise, sex does not indicate an intimate relationship. An intimate relationship means studying the other person; learning his or her bents, strengths, and desires; living in a participatory and understanding manner; working together. Just as simply applying for citizenship won't cut it in France, so joining two bodies together won't make two people intimate. If that were true then prostitutes would be the most intimate people in the world.

The Lord says that moral excellence is required to begin the process of intimacy. Premarital sex is *not* moral excellence. If a marriage has its roots in premarital sex, a new covenant of excellence needs to be established, and a new citizenship applied for. This citizenship rests in the divine covenant of Christ. If we have knowledge of the saving grace of Christ yet think lightly of it and His divine sacrifice, we will neither seek love nor obtain it, because we will not understand it.

I didn't understand Christ's love for me when I filed for a divorce. I didn't understand how terribly I had betrayed Him with my sin, and that He yet loved me. My love was based solely on what I understood—my own needs and pleasures. And at the time, my greatest need was to stop the fighting.

Something remarkable happened, though, when I filed for a divorce. Brian and I both got the wind knocked out of us. When we met in a public place to talk about the divorce papers, we didn't burn with anger. We were calm.

I had moved back in with my parents, and occasionally Brian

would call me. Our conversations seemed different. They had an element of concern. As the months dragged on, and the court date to finalize our divorce loomed nearer, we saw each other from time to time and never fought.

I am not sure what made the change come about. Perhaps it was God's mercy acting on two hearts that were defeated. Love and trust had not been restored, but the hate had begun to dissipate. The thought occurred to me that I would be going ahead with a divorce simply because I wanted out.

I had made the decision to divorce amid emotional upheavals and a desire for peace. Now I was thinking clearly, and we were behaving a bit more congenially. I thought, *How can I knowingly break God's commandment against divorce simply because I want out of my marriage?* Although my relationship with God was tenuous at the time, and neither Brian nor I were going to church, I knew enough from recent experience that willingly breaking God's commandments would result in dire consequences. Would fear of God be enough of a foundation to hold my marriage together?

Brian had signed the papers months earlier, but all along he had said he was opposed to the divorce. I knew he would agree if I called it off. My thoughts turned to our daughter. She was only eight months old. Was I going to affect her life so drastically simply because I didn't want to care anymore for her daddy? These and other questions consumed me in the last few weeks leading up to our court date.

The separation had given me time to think, and in that time I realized I wanted to do what was right even if doing right didn't agree with my feelings. I hoped that the right emotions would come later. In living through the consequences of my sinfulness and selfishness, my fear of God had grown. I was too afraid to divorce and risk chastisement again. So I called off the divorce a few weeks before it was to become final.

After I moved back into our home the fights, although they still occurred, were less frequent. I think we realized, at last, that we needed to *work* at this relationship. Before our separation, the possibility of a divorce had kept me from controlling much of my anger. I had, at times, thought that if I made Brian mad enough he would leave me and then I wouldn't have the responsibility of filing. I could blame him and comfort myself with "poor me." Once divorce was no longer an option, I tried to accept things that I didn't like. The finality of a divorce shocked us both out of focusing solely on ourselves. It scared us and woke us up to things we needed to change.

We started going to a Christian marriage counselor who helped us understand what a Christian marriage should look like. We also started watching a preacher on the television each Sunday. At first it was hard, because we had gotten out of the habit of hearing someone speak of spiritual things. It was almost like a foreign language. Brian says he literally forced himself to listen because he knew it was the right thing to do; I followed suit. It seemed like all the preacher ever talked about, though, was Jesus' forgiveness and His death on the cross. That's exactly what Brian and I both needed to hear. After a few months of hearing about the love of Jesus and making efforts to be more kind, we found our anger slowly subsiding.

Then, as part of a course assignment, my college drama class put on a Christmas play. It was the winter that Brian and I celebrated our second wedding anniversary. Each group was responsible for its own material. I'm ashamed to admit that my group's skit wasn't spiritual in the least, but there was another group that was made up of Christians. They did something very simple for their skit, but it was life changing for me.

When it came time for the program, all five of them sat on the stage and took turns reciting different portions of a story written by Max Lucado. The piece, from Lucado's book *God Came Near,* was about Jesus' incarnation. Lucado's words painted a picture of Jesus I had never seen before. This Jesus was approachable, yet divine. He was holy, yet humble. I was mesmerized. I had to get that book. After reading it and other books by Max Lucado, I wanted to get back into church. I wanted to get to know this Jesus personally. Brian also began to read the books I had bought, and his heart was drawn to God. I remember one time when Brian was reading, I looked over at him and saw he had goose bumps on his arms. I asked him what was up, and he said, "This guy writes like you're standing in the very room with Jesus. It's as if I'm there. . . . It's amazing!"

So we decided to go back to church on Sunday mornings—but just *church,* mind you. We weren't comfortable enough to join a small group. So we went to church and sat in the back row. We also bought more Christian books to read during the week. And I started to pray for grace and mercy. At the time, that's all I could think of to pray for. I now know that many others, especially my mom, had been faithfully praying for us during that time and long before.

Our premature marriage had had a sickly start, and our hearts had been ready to pull the plug on it. But unbeknownst to us, God had been at work. He had been nursing our marriage as if it were in an incubator. All that time, it had been in a place of healing warmed by His grace.

6

Despoiling the Temple

During the time when the Old Testament temple was being built, a single king ruled all twelve tribes of Israel. Not long after it was completed, the king died, and his son took his place. The twelve tribes soon became dissatisfied with their new king, and they asked him, for one thing, to go easier on taxes. The king thought about their request and sought advice. Then he responded foolishly. He said no.

Leaders of ten of the tribes left the king's palace that day and went back to their towns. Once there, they said they wanted a new king. The new king of the ten tribes was Jeroboam, and he ruled in the northern kingdom of Israel. Another king ruled the southern kingdom from Jerusalem, where the temple was located.

Jeroboam, tough though he was, soon became fearful. He realized that God would require his people to worship at the temple in Jerusalem. He reasoned, "If this people go up to offer sacrifices in the house of the LORD at Jerusalem, then the heart of this people will return to their lord, even to Rehoboam king of Judah; and they will kill me and return to Rehoboam king of Judah" (1 Kings 12:27).

So Jeroboam made a substitute god. He ordered the making of

two golden calves, and he then said to the people, "'It is too much for you to go up to Jerusalem; behold your gods, O Israel, that brought you up from the land of Egypt.' And he set one in Bethel, and the other he put in Dan. Now this thing became a sin" (1 Kings 12:28–30).

Jeroboam hoped that, by offering a cheap substitute for the altar in Jerusalem, he would prosper. He was wrong. His sin resulted in a loss of fellowship with God and a loss of blessing from Him.

Cheap substitutes come in a variety of forms. Premarital sex became for me a cheap substitute for God's design of authentic intimacy. Satan held out the fruit of "free sex" under the false promise that I could benefit without making the covenant of marriage. Yet cheap substitutes eventually show their deficiencies as they produce grave results.

The Lord spoke many things to Jeroboam's wife, telling of the personal destruction that Jeroboam and his ancestors would face because of his "other gods and molten images." Beyond the physical results, though, lies the direst result of all—the spiritual separation from God's blessings. God said, "[I] will give up Israel on account of the sins of Jeroboam, which he committed and with which he made Israel to sin" (1 Kings 14:16).

Similarly, in the case of premarital sex, spiritual consequences occur as well. Premarital sex doesn't begin in the bedroom. It begins in the heart (see Matt. 5:27–28; 15:19–20). This is the same heart that God tells us to circumcise and guard. It is the same heart with which God tells us to draw near to Him and make melody. Elevating Brian and myself above God in my heart was elevating our relationship to the level of idolatry.

The Bible is clear on God's command against idolatry: "Thou shall have no other gods before me." A *god* in Bible times was often an idol made of wood, stone, or gold. People appealed to their gods for, among other things, food, happiness, and prosperity. Today, our gods don't always come carved in the shape of a specific object. They might be people, establishments, recreations, or ideas that we turn to for fulfillment.

When deciding to engage in premarital sex, the god might be you—your own desires, pleasures, or worth. Or it can be something else—your peers, your boyfriend/girlfriend, or even a romantic notion. God responded to Jeroboam's idolatry with disaster. He said, "I will make a clean sweep of the house of Jeroboam, as one sweeps away dung until it is all gone" (1 Kings 14:10). God has every right to respond as harshly to our idolatry today. He is perfectly just in excising idolatry out of the recesses of our souls. He often does this through consequences or what is, for a believer, called chastisement.

"The severity of the operation is caused by the depth of the malady to be cured," writes Fenelon, the archbishop of Cambria around the turn of the eighteenth century. "God would not cut if there were no sore. He only probes the ulcerated proud flesh. So, after all, it is our own noxious self-will which is the cause of what we suffer."[1]

During the time that I wrongly elevated Brian and myself through premarital sex, I felt ambiguous about what it was I was doing. Idolatry or a form of pride was the last thing I considered it to be. The thought never crossed my mind. Even after we had gotten married and God allowed many relational hardships to cut away at me, I delayed repenting of my sin for years. Of course, I told God I was sorry on multiple occasions during that time, but it was years before I spoke from my heart as well as from my lips. Repentance meant admitting that what I had done was wrong. I had merely been expressing sorrow that I'd gotten caught.

It was so easy to rationalize my choice. Since Brian and I had talked about getting married some day, the first time we had sex I told myself that we had simply consummated our marriage early. After that first time, we even told each other, "God considers us married now." Rationalizing our sin reduced our feelings of guilt.

Blinding myself to the holiness of God and His righteous justice, I took comfort in ignorance. To acknowledge the just character of God would have only magnified my guilt.

This blindness carried over into my spiritual life. I remained on a surface level of fellowship with God and enjoyed no real intimacy with Jesus. To go deeper or to move closer would require a change of heart about my sin. I didn't want to do that because my sin simulated a fulfilling of my legitimate need for intimacy and satisfied my felt needs for control and excitement. To admit that I had been rationalizing would be to admit I had been deceived and was foolish. And that my needs really hadn't been met after all.

The problem with my rationalization was that I could not deny the invalidity of our consummation. Legally, Brian and I were not one before our marriage. I could have left Brian during this time of premarital sex at any time with no legal ramifications. I could have married someone else without first having the stain of a divorce. Nor did Brian and I share any mutual responsibilities while unmarried. If he bothered me one day, I could simply tell him I wanted to be alone, and he would have to leave. If he left his clothes out all over his room, I didn't care because I didn't share his room. If I grumbled with PMS, he could simply return to his dorm for the next few days. We desired one another yet we were both disposable, depending on how we felt.

In marriage, however, commitment means neither partner is disposable. Commitment carries relationships through the mundane and the bothersome. True commitment is a lifelong vow before the Creator, not merely an obligation before others.

A look at marriage in Scripture gives a better understanding of the significance of commitment within a covenant as opposed to mere desires and intentions. Consider the marriage between Jacob—the son of Isaac and grandson of Abraham—and Leah.

When Jacob fled from his angry brother and went to stay at his uncle Laban's home, he fell in love with Laban's daughter Rachel. Laban told Jacob that he could marry Rachel in return for seven years of labor. When it came time for the wedding, Laban tricked Jacob. Following the ceremony, when the bride's veil was removed, Jacob found he had become married to Rachel's sister, Leah.

Jacob didn't want to marry Leah. His heart longed to marry Rachel. His intention, during his seven years of labor, was to marry Rachel. Yet, neither his heart nor his previous intention could change the fact that he had, instead, made a covenant with Leah. Realizing this, Jacob assumed the role of husband to Leah.

Intentions don't mean much compared to covenants. Yet I had based my justification for having sex with Brian solely on an intention. It was as if I had taken and then eaten a candy bar with the intention of purchasing it later. I could get the sugary taste now without having to sacrifice anything for it.

I actually tried to do that —sort of—when I was four. I didn't really intend to buy the candy bar myself, but I did intend for my mom to buy it. I had just forgotten to ask her. When I got to the car and went to open the wrapper, my mom asked me where I had gotten the candy. When I told her, she quickly marched me back into the store to return it. I had intended all along for my mom to pay for it, but the store owner didn't care for a moment about what I had intended. He wanted his candy bar back or the payment for it. No matter what my intentions, I had stolen.

When I chose to engage in premarital sex, I willfully destroyed the sanctity of a dimension of Brian's life and my life by exalting my wants and desires, along with Brian's wants and desires, above God's. Scripture tells us to "Flee immorality. Every other sin that a man commits is outside the body, but the immoral man sins against his own body" (1 Cor. 6:18). All sin interrupts the fellowship between people and God. Sexual sin, however, is unique in that the very things used in sinning, our bodies, are the things that God desires to indwell with His Spirit. Sins such as coveting grieve our Father, but physical immorality mocks Him. Jesus bought my body with a price—His death on the cross. When I wrongfully gave my body to Brian, I gave something that was not mine.

In no other Scripture passage do we find Jesus so livid as when He overturned the sellers' tables in the temple. At that time, the temple was where God had chosen to dwell. His temple was to be a house of prayer, a place for communion with Him. But the vendors in the temple had turned it into a place to make money, right under God's nose.

Today, "*We* are the temple of the living God" (2 Cor. 6:16, emphasis added). His Spirit dwells within us. God doesn't leave while we commit a sin and return when we are done. We deeply grieve the Holy Spirit when we sin.

I once experienced a hint of the grievousness of using the dwelling place of the Spirit for personal gain. A few years after Brian and I were married I returned to college. We decided to take a short trip together, but since we were both in college we didn't have much money. We scraped together enough for a two-day excursion, but we lacked any extra for spending.

One day, before our trip, I saw an ad in the campus paper offering to buy blood plasma. I knew that other college students often sold their plasma. *It couldn't be that bad,* I reasoned. *I probably have enough plasma to go around. The extra cash would be nice.*

I drove to the donation center feeling little hesitation. Yet as they hooked me up to the mammoth machines, I began to get uneasy. I felt as if I was an extra in an Orson Wells science fiction movie. The room smelled like a box of moldy Comet. Blood circulated in full view through the huge tunnels in the machines next to each person. Rows of beds lined each wall, and everyone lying in them stared straight ahead, their faces expressionless.

My face, on the other hand, became tense. After only twenty

minutes, I began to tremble. My skin crawled with shivers. Then I started to cry, weep actually, which in a room full of strangers was humiliating. But, still attached to the machine, I had to wait it out for another hour—tears, trembles, and all. The nurse monitoring me called Brian at our home and told him to come and get me.

Later, as I left with money in hand, I struggled to understand what had happened and why I had reacted so intensely. Even though I had gone voluntarily, I felt violated. Then it hit me that I was *selling* my body. Donating blood seemed different because that was giving of myself for the benefit of another. I wasn't profiting from it. Yet, in this case, I had literally sold a part of my body. It was a disgusting realization. I was convinced that I had dishonored God.

God has chosen to indwell the bodies that He bought with a price. Whatever we do should be based on the realization that we are not our own. Otherwise, we wind up with guilt and regret. Guilt comes from the Holy Spirit, whose job is to convict us of sin. Although guilt should never remain once we've been forgiven, it is a good indicator that we need to seek forgiveness.

Gary Thomas, a Christian author and former college pastor, says that when students on his campus used to come to him with grief and shame over something they had done in the past, it never had to do with stealing, lying, or cheating—they had no problem receiving forgiveness for these sins; no flashbacks filled with angst. Shame usually meant the sin had something to do with a sin against the body.[2]

Sins against the body include abusing drugs and alcohol, engaging in immoral sex, and abortion. Sins against the body are different from other sins—they are committed against God's very temple, and they are committed against our very selves. They are acts of degradation and desecration against our own bodies.

Sins against the body, too, are more difficult to forget, because they include all five senses. Premarital sex involves the sense of touch, taste, sight, hearing, and smell. The sexual act encompasses all of our sensory elements and does so at an intense level. Little wonder, then, that sins against the body leave a lasting effect.

The effects are not only emotional and physical, they are spiritual as well—because our bodies are not our own. God owns first, and only, rights to the bodies of Christians. Our bodies are His. He bought and paid for them at a very high price. Sinning against one's own body, then, is akin to undervaluing one's worth and selling oneself far too cheaply.

To illustrate, I gave an assignment to my high school students, asking them to submit one of their written pieces to a publisher. On the cover page, they were to put what "rights" they were offering the publisher. They could offer first, simultaneous, or all rights.

First rights means that the article could be sold again after it was published. *Simultaneous rights* means that the article could be sold again even while it was being published. *All rights* means that, without prior written permission from the publisher, the article couldn't even be printed in a church newsletter. Publishers purchasing all rights, however, pay more.

When Jesus redeemed us with His blood, He paid a high price for all rights. He bought all rights to us whether or not we relinquish all of ourselves to Him. We cannot simultaneously do whatever we choose with our bodies, minds, or hearts. Nor can we enjoy His benefits first, only to sell ourselves later to another person. Christ's contract says He gets all. When we don't willingly give Him our "all," we are breaking His command to "love the Lord your God with *all* your heart, and with *all* your soul, and with *all* your strength, and with *all* your mind" (Luke 10:27, emphasis added).

Breaking God's commands means that we have not only sinned and are in need of forgiveness but that also we have offended our intimate relationship with Him. Sins against God, denied and unaddressed, fester and carry spiritual consequences that further challenge marital intimacy. Spiritual consequences are separation from God, decreased usefulness, doubt in regard to spiritual leadership in the home, anger toward God and others.

Separation from God

"But your iniquities have made a separation between you and your God, and your sins have hidden His face from you, so that He does not hear" (Isa. 59:2). Sin separates us from the Father. It can even stop God from hearing us.

I was raised in an era of independence and positive self-esteem curricula, all of which nurture self-centeredness. When I sinned by engaging in premarital sex I assumed that, rather than God rejecting me, I had rejected the Father. Since I had walked away, I believed I could return to Him however I pleased.

While I could return to Him *whenever* I pleased, I couldn't return to Him *however* I pleased. My return needed to be accompanied by a change of heart. Despite the fact that God was not the one who walked away, it was He who set the terms for my return.

In the book of Hosea, when the Israelites pursued their own pleasures in preference to knowing God, Jehovah said through the prophet, "My people are destroyed for lack of knowledge. Because you have rejected knowledge, I also will reject you from being My priest. Since you have forgotten the law of your God, I also will forget your children" (4:6).

Knowledge refers to knowledge of God (see v. 1). A lack of knowledge, or godly fear, resulted in the Israelites' sin. God's holiness forbids Him from remaining with sin. God, the Father, leaves. We don't. Hosea continues, "They will go with their flocks and their herds to seek the LORD, but they will not find Him; *He has withdrawn from them*" (5:6, emphasis added).

Even when Israel sought God following their sin, they could

not find Him. Even when Israel traveled to the true altar to meet God, He was not there—until they sought Him with humbled and broken hearts (see v. 15).

After my sin had become public I, like Israel, repeatedly sought God's forgiveness and fellowship. But because of, among other things, pride and selfishness, I didn't seek those things the way God desires—with a humbled and honest heart. I sought God's forgiveness because I wanted out of the mess that my relationships had turned into. I sought His forgiveness because I had been caught. I didn't seek His forgiveness out of a reverence for who He was. As a result, during all of that time, I didn't receive the peace God promises upon repentance.

Decreased Usefulness

Recently I offered Michael, a youth at my church, a drink of juice to illustrate a biblical point in our lesson. In one hand I offered it to him in a beautifully crafted, authentic German goblet. In the other, I offered him the juice in a peanut butter jar. Michael chose the peanut butter jar. He did so because, prior to the class, I had rubbed oil in and around the goblet and then covered the inside with dirt. I had also carefully washed the peanut butter jar.

While the goblet may have outwardly resembled majesty, its inward filth made it undesirable for use. While the peanut butter jar may have outwardly appeared ordinary, its inward cleanliness made it desirable for use.[3]

The Pharisees of Jesus' day represented, too, a dichotomy in outward and inward cleanliness. Outwardly, the Pharisees maintained appearances by regularly attending synagogue and adhering to respected traditions and commandments. Yet, inwardly, their hearts reflected loyalty to none but themselves. Jesus rebuked them, "Woe to you, scribes and Pharisees, hypocrites! For you clean the outside of the cup and of the dish . . . first clean the inside of the cup and of the dish, so that the outside of it may become clean also" (Matt. 23:25–26).

My sin of premarital sex, when not repented of, stained my soul, making me as desirable to God for His use as was the filthy goblet to Michael. It wasn't until I returned to be cleansed by Him that I experienced the grace that comes from being used by God. Unfortunately, that was four years later than it should have been.

Doubt in Regard to Spiritual Leadership in the Home

Premarital sex also affected the spiritual dynamics of our home. I realize now that God, in designing marriage, intended that the husband should be the head in the relationship. Yet even when I didn't realize this, the need was present within Brian's heart. Men innately desire respect in their leadership roles.

Our indulgence in premarital sex, however, meant ultimately, among other things, that Brian had compromised morality for immediate gratification. When faced with this reality, after we married I withheld respect and trust for Brian in all areas of his leadership in our home. I questioned, *If he has compromised here, where will he compromise later? Will there be something he desires, now that we're married, for which he will compromise? How do I know his decisions are based on what is right rather than on his own pleasure?*

This doubt about spiritual leadership in our home lay primarily in the areas of judgment and service. I found it difficult to trust Brian's judgments. Brian found it difficult to trust the motive behind my volunteer services outside the home. He had seen how easily I had compromised morality to obtain fulfillment before. When I later worked as a spokesperson for a Christian organization, Brian hesitated to encourage me. Rather, he questioned my motive. *Is Heather's motive really to help the people in the organiza-tion, or is it to fulfill some need within her?* His doubts led to many disagreements about the division of my time, and our doubts about one another produced massive disunity in our home.

Because sexual fulfillment had tempted us into making a poor judgment based on a wrong motive, we now questioned each other's every motive. But beyond that, we questioned each other's wis-dom. When it came time for Brian to make a family decision or to give me advice, I automatically dismissed what he said. My thoughts didn't consciously examine past events, nor did I verbally question Brian. The rejection was a knee-jerk reaction. It became difficult for him to lead when I refused to follow.

I wrote to a friend, for example, about some new things God was teaching me concerning prayer. I asked for her thoughts. Re-ally liking her response, I shared it with Brian. Halfway through reading it, though, I realized her thoughts were similar to those Brian had expressed all along. He realized it too.

"Why didn't you listen to me?" he asked. "I've said the same thing for years."

"Ummm . . . uh . . ." I didn't know what to say.

I had become so self-protective in my reactions to Brian that I had refused to grow and risk trust. Brian isn't the same person he was when we first married as teenagers. Neither am I. Yet out of self-preservation, we subconsciously often relate to each other as if we were those same people. Having experienced the painful con-sequences of premarital sex, we find it more difficult to risk trust-ing each other's motives and decisions.

Anger Toward God and Others

This is tough to acknowledge. We like to assume that our anger toward others is justified and that our anger toward God doesn't exist. Sure, we all get annoyed by other people from time to time (okay . . . daily) simply because we are human. But, in reality, our annoyance doesn't reveal the faults of others as much as it reveals our own sinfulness.

Years after our wedding, and a long time after I thought I had worked through my resentments, Brian and I sat in with a small group of couples who are in full-time ministry and who are roughly our age. I was not used to being with people our age. Because of the ages of our children and the young age at which we bore them, Brian and I have normally been grouped with couples who are considerably older than we are.

The group was participating in an icebreaker activity. Each couple was to create a collage together that was to reflect the story of their marriage—what they liked to do together, how they met, significant events in their relationships. I suddenly grew impatient with everyone, and my blood began to boil. I had to leave the room. *This is strange,* I thought. I'm a phlegmatic person, and normally I enjoy watching other people entertain themselves.

When I returned, I looked at all the other couples. They were laughing and enjoying this time of reminiscing. Then I looked at Brian. He, too, seemed to be enjoying himself as he cut and pasted pictures representing our children and our hobbies. *Why am I reacting this way?* I wondered.

The girl sitting next to me, who is now a friend, nearly drove me nuts. She and her husband had been married just under four years, yet I was convinced they were still on their honeymoon. Their first and only child was just eight months old and was, of course, perfect—as firstborns tend to be. They had spent thousands of dollars on their wedding and shared countless hours of joyful anticipation and preparation. I was sitting next to Mr. and Mrs. Ken and Barbie Live-Happily-Ever-After.

If only . . . I thought. If only we had known then what we know

now. We would have waited until we were married to have sex. We, like these others, would have cherished the beginning of our family and the precious time that comes with a firstborn. Instead, we had been distracted by so many changes and emotions. We surely wouldn't have said so many immature and hurtful things to each other. I would have taken an early interest in Brian and his growth and encouraged him rather than viewing him as a competitor for time and resources.

I was jealous of the happiness the other couples enjoyed. When I realized it, I was ashamed. Though I made it through the collage, I didn't make any friends in the process that day, which was part of the reason for doing it. Later as I drove through town, I cried. I asked God, "Why didn't you stop us? Why didn't you prevent us? Why didn't you send Josh McDowell five years earlier to challenge the youth of America to 'wait'? We would have listened!"

I had never verbally blamed God for anything before. I shuddered at my audacity and waited for the bolt of lightning. God wasn't the one at fault here. But I accused, and the lightning never came. Rather, the words "I forgive you," slipped from my lips. I said them again, "I forgive you." I couldn't believe what I was saying. God hadn't done anything wrong. I knew that. So what on earth was I forgiving *Him* for? He didn't need to be forgiven, but I needed to forgive. So I did. I forgave Him for my disappointments, confusion, and my consequences. In essence, I acknowledged that He was just in it all.

Our second child is emotional and gets upset when things go wrong because of sin. During those times she often cries and says, "I wish that God had never made Satan in the first place!" She reasons that if Satan hadn't tempted Eve to sin we would live in heaven now.

We explain to her that God chose to allow Satan to do what he did and for reasons beyond our own understanding. We also explain that our being saved from sin glorifies God and that Satan is not the sole source of temptation—we have our own sinful flesh with which to contend as well.

For our daughter to remain angry with God would be harmful to her. Who else can she turn to for perfect strength and love? Yet anger at God is sometimes our immediate reaction when we're confronted with the consequences of sin or with the awareness of our own sinfulness. However wrong anger at God is, it does occur. Denying it doesn't make it any less wrong. And unless we deal with it by acknowledging both the sovereignty of a just and holy God and our own sinful natures, that anger will continue to separate us from Him.

The forgiveness I gave to God that day in the car ultimately fell on someone else other than Him. I had only directed it to Him because He was the one I'd been blaming all along. Really, though, it was myself I forgave, because on some level I was recognizing my own culpability.

From that day on, a weight slowly lifted from me. I was no longer angry at the thought that other people engaged in premarital sex and didn't get caught. God had reminded me that He is in control, that my disappointments and shame are to His glory when they, through forgiveness, reveal the depths of His grace. In His reproofs, He chisels away at character to reveal a humble and grateful heart.

I got to know the couples in our collage-making group over the next few months. As I did, I saw that no matter what we all look like on the outside—even if we are in full-time Christian ministry—there really isn't a Mr. and Mrs. Ken and Barbie Live-Happily-Ever-After. Every couple experiences struggles. If our struggles push us either individually or as couples into a more intimate relationship with God, then our struggles are a blessing.

Consider the only survivor of a shipwreck, who was washed up on a small, uninhabited island. He prayed feverishly for God to rescue him, and every day he scanned the horizon for help, but none seemed forthcoming.

He eventually managed to build a little hut out of driftwood to protect him from the elements, and in which to store his few possessions. But one day, exhausted from scavenging for food, he arrived home to find his little hut in flames, the smoke rolling up to the sky. The worst had happened; everything was lost. He was stunned with grief and anger. "God, how could you do this to me!" he cried.

Early the next day, however, he was awakened by the sound of a ship as it approached the island. It had come to rescue him. "How did you know I was here?" asked the weary man of his rescuers.

"We saw your smoke signal," they replied.

Understand, friend, that even smoke signals from a burning pyre of sin can evoke the attention, care, and deliverance of an all-knowing God.

Do not let discouragement smother the flame of hope. Rather put your hope in the One who can help you reclaim the intimacy that has been lost.

Section 3

Reclaiming Intimacy

7

I Repent

On a table in my bedroom sits a framed picture of our wedding. The picture shows Brian and me kneeling before an altar and a large wooden cross. When my son was two years old, he took a red crayon and drew all over the white doors in my bedroom. He also drew on my wedding picture—a circle all the way around the cross. I haven't the heart to wipe it off. He did, after all, circle the most important thing.

Any married couple seeking to reclaim or reestablish intimacy in their relationship must also begin with a red mark. They must build their union under the blood of Jesus on the cross. Jesus, who is the source of all things, is the source of intimacy as well. "The Father loves the Son, and has given *all things* into His hands" (John 3:35, emphasis added). Not only does Jesus hold our eternal life in His hands, He also holds the truest expression of our desires in our earthly lives.

Jesus is life. Jesus is intimacy. Jesus is total satisfaction. Beside Him there is none other. Jesus will reclaim the intimacy in your marriage, as He is doing in mine. Without Him, I have as much chance for authentic intimacy as does a schoolchild with a crush on her teacher. She desires her teacher's affection but in no way can obtain it. In a marriage, only through Jesus is the playing field made level and intimacy obtainable. Because in Him all things are true and pure, and conversely, in everyone else nothing is true and pure.

Yet the One who holds all things is the One I betrayed when I chose to engage in premarital sex. I betrayed His commands and the blood He shed for my sins. I can never make up for what I did, or for what I still do when I sin. But—there is something I can do.

The path to perfect intimacy begins with the first stepping stone laid by Jesus. That stepping stone is called repentance. I can take a step onto that stone by repenting. The Greek word that has been translated in Scripture as "repentance" means literally to "change your mind." Repentance is not guilt, remorse, or even sorrow. While these things may lead to repentance, repentance itself involves a mental change of direction. "To repent is to alter one's way of looking at life; it is to take God's point of view instead of one's own." Repentance means changing my mind about my actions, confessing that they are in opposition to the revealed will of God, and admitting ownership of my sin.

Each of us has an innate desire to protect ourselves, and this desire often is manifested in blame. Blame has existed as long as sin. After Adam ate the forbidden fruit in the Garden of Eden, he defended himself to God: "The woman *you* put here with me— she gave me some fruit from the tree" (Gen. 3:12 NIV, emphasis added). Adam played the blame-game on his very first offense.

Ownership means acknowledging our participation in sin, despite the external influences that might contribute to our behavior. Repentance means that I have to set aside the *victim* mentality and declare myself the *perpetrator.*

I was not a victim of ignorance, lust, or my emotions. I was not a victim of my culture or my environment. My sin was my doing, and it was my fault. I didn't make a *mistake.* I didn't do something *accidentally.* Premarital sex wasn't just an *unwise action.* It was *sin.*

Not until I honestly acknowledged that every bit of pleasure, fulfillment, and esteem I had gained through premarital sex was stolen at the expense of my Savior was I truly repentant. Repentance involved a change of mind about what I had done and, in so doing, left no room for residual pleasure through memories or associated emotions.

Repentance also involved more than selfish sorrow. I had told God I was sorry on numerous occasions before I actually repented. But my regret stemmed from disappointments in the consequences my sin had created, not in my horror of perpetrating an offense so appalling.

Against whom did I perpetrate this sin? For a long time I thought it was against Brian, my parents, my future children, and myself. Following his sexual sin with Bathsheba, David wrote, "Against Thee, Thee only, I have sinned, and done what is evil in Thy sight" (Ps. 51:4).

My sin, too, had been perpetrated against God, and until I recognized that fact I could not truly repent. Andrew Murray challenges us to acknowledge against whom we sin, when we sin:

> How much awakened sinners concentrate their thoughts simply on the views that they have sinned against themselves and their own happiness, and how little on what ought to cause them the greatest concern, namely, the fact that they have sinned against God. . . . Is He not the King and Lawgiver of heaven and earth, whose will is joyfully accomplished throughout the whole heaven . . . against this God you have sinned; that is, you have withheld obedience from Him. You have refused to do what He has commanded you. You have not hesitated to violate and break

His holy law. You have sinned against Him. You have ex-
alted and chosen your will, unjust and perverse as it is,
above His will. You have said that the counsel of Satan is
more attractive to you and has more influence with you
than the will of God. . . . You, a poor worm of the dust,
you have affronted and insulted the high and holy One
before whom angels prostrate themselves.[1]

Healing can begin in the home only after sin is dealt with in the
heavens. Authentic intimacy in our relationships can come only
after we recognize that the One we have betrayed is the One who
loves us the most—God.

For years I tried to minimize my sin of premarital sex by using
my age and circumstances as excuses. I even diminished it in my
mind—I had premarital sex with only one person while others
have premarital sex with multiple partners throughout their lives.
Minimizing my sin only removed my felt-need for heartfelt repentance. A dangerous circumstance. By not repenting, I crippled my
intimacy with Brian as well as my intimacy with God. And it ate
away at my life.

A similar thing happened to King David. David did not repent
of his sexual sin with Bathsheba for nearly a year. He writes concerning that period of time, "When I kept silent about my sin, my
body wasted away." His body wasted away under the strain of his
sinfulness. His spirit wasted away because the source of His life
was cut off.

Being from Generation X, I have an aversion to the word *repentance*. It flies in the face of independence and autonomy, things we
Xers feel entitled to and continually strive for. The very word *repentance* sounds archaic and needy. It even sounds stoic—an action performed through sheer will. Yet denying my need for
repentance only leads to loneliness. What good is autonomy when

it isolates you? Repentance also requires an honest comparison of my views with God's Word. In comparing them, I can be anything but stoic. It is incredibly heart breaking, humbling, humiliating, and sad.

The good thing is that repentance leads to the next stepping stone on the path toward authentic intimacy—the stepping stone of peace. "If you're dealing with unconfessed moral sins," says Dr. Tony Evans, "then that's why you have no joy. That's why you have no peace. That's why you have no power, no sense of God's presence, and your prayers are not being answered. Because when you don't come right with God, He doesn't hang out with you."[2]

Pleasure may produce a temporary satisfaction, but it never produces peace. Only repentance leads to peace. Consider Peter and Judas. Both sinned against Jesus. One betrayed Him, and the other denied Him. Both expressed remorse, yet Judas will forever be known as the betrayer while Peter is the apostle with power. Why?

The reason rests with the difference between remorse and repentance. Remorse is defined as "a gnawing distress arising from a sense of guilt for past wrongs."[3] This gnawing distress dead-ends in self-reproach while repentance leads to life.

Shortly after Jesus was delivered to Pilate, following Judas's betrayal in the garden, Judas's heart was filled with remorse. "When Judas, who had betrayed Him, saw that He had been condemned, he felt remorse" (Matt. 27:3). Judas may not have expected the chief priests and elders to actually condemn Jesus to death but simply to imprison Him. Or maybe Judas thought Jesus would fight to establish His kingdom. Whatever he thought, Judas now "saw that [Jesus] had been condemned" (v. 3).

In Judaism, contributing to the shedding of innocent blood is equated with murder. Because Jesus was innocent of any crime, turning Him over to the authorities to be killed would, at the very least, create in Judas's mind a death sentence on himself. According to the Old Testament law, a murderer's guilt could be atoned by nothing less than his or her own blood.[4]

Because Jesus had been condemned Judas was filled with remorse. He saw the consequences of his sin. Judas's remorse led to confession. There is no record, however, of that confession being directed to God. Rather, he spoke to those in human authority over him. "He . . . returned the thirty pieces of silver to the chief priests and elders, saying, 'I have sinned by betraying innocent blood'" (vv. 3–4).

The very next verse goes on to tell us that Judas's remorse led to death. "And he threw the pieces of silver into the sanctuary and departed; and he went away and hanged himself" (v. 5). Luke later writes, "And falling headlong, [Judas] burst open in the middle and all his bowels gushed out" (Acts 1:18). Remorse had left Judas literally empty.

Now consider Peter. Peter denied knowing Jesus three times, although earlier Peter had told Jesus he would never deny Him. Yet, just as remorse may lead to an empty death, repentance leads to life.

When Peter realized what he had done, "he went out and wept bitterly" (Matt. 26:75). It's recorded that both Peter and Judas felt sorry for their sins and expressed their sorrow earnestly. Judas returned the silver, and Peter wept bitterly. Yet repentance involves a change of mind that "promotes a change in the course being pursued."[5] Peter's change of mind was evidenced when he later no longer feared others more than God. When Peter heard that Jesus wasn't in the tomb he ran to it, even though, as far as he knew, there were still Roman soldiers guarding it. Peter ran with the hope of seeing his Savior. He didn't run away to hide. He went to the One he had denied.

Later when Jesus came to His disciples at the Sea of Galilee, Peter jumped into the water and swam a hundred yards to meet

Him. Then when Jesus asked Peter if he loved Him, Peter replied, "Lord, you know all things. You know I do." Following Jesus' ascension, Peter risked his own life, standing before the council and high priest. Although he had been forbidden to do so, Peter had taught in the name of Jesus. He spoke boldly, "We must obey God rather than men" (Acts 5:29).

Judas and Peter both realized that they had sinned. We are told that both felt sorrow. Yet only Peter's remorse led to repentance, effectuating a change of mind about himself and prompting a change in his actions. Only Peter's response led to peace.

A number of years later, the apostle Paul wrote to those who had been brought to repentance through his chastising words, "I now rejoice, not that you were made sorrowful, but that you were made sorrowful to the point of repentance; for you were made sorrowful according to the will of God. . . . For the sorrow that is according to the will of God produces a repentance without regret, leading to salvation; but the sorrow of the world produces death" (2 Cor. 7:9–10).

Godly sorrow produces "repentance without regret." It produces repentance without shame and without guilt. A popular Christian song goes, "I'm reeling from these voices that keep screaming in my ears. All these words of shame and doubt, blame and regret . . . while You're up there just playing hard to get."[6]

Yet it isn't God who plays hard to get. Rather, it is we who play hard to give. Early on in my marriage, I didn't want to get close enough to God to truly trust Him. To trust God meant I needed to know Him. To know God meant I had to come face-to-face with who He is. And His holiness undid me, because I was so far removed from obedience or humility. God's holiness even undid Isaiah, a man who had spent his life seeking to obey God. The first five chapters of the book of Isaiah are filled with "woes" of condemnation against the Israelites for sinning. Yet in chapter six, when Isaiah records seeing God's holiness himself, he can only say, "Woe is *me!*" (Isa. 6:5, emphasis added). His proclamation of woe became directed at himself.

It's easy to say, "Woe is me" over personal pains or relationship problems. *Boo-hoo.* I forget, though, *why* I should say, "Woe is me." I should say *woe* in response to God's glory. I hesitated to do so, crouching behind a shield of pride.

Instead of trusting God and leaving myself entirely to Him, I chose early on to view Him as I do the Siberian tiger at the zoo. I am in awe of the tiger's awesome power, so I observe him through the protection of glass a foot thick. I can still imagine I'm fairly strong as long as I stay outside the glass. Yet if I were to step inside, into the presence of the tiger, I would discover how weak I really am. Rather than take that risk, I stay behind the glass barrier. I put my trust in the glass.

God, of course, is not a tiger who is only to be feared. Rather, God is just yet merciful. He can be trusted. God wants us to *fear* and *trust* Him at the same time. Our fear and awe of who He really is aligns our thoughts with His. Our trust in Him turns our expectations away from others and toward the One who is supremely trustworthy.

When I changed my mind concerning God's holiness and my sinfulness, I placed myself solely at His mercy. I stepped beyond the glass shield of pride and doubt and into the presence of the awesome God. King David cried, I fell "into the hand of the LORD for His mercies are great" (2 Sam. 24:14). It is the safest place to be.

It is also the most peaceful.

In Old Testament times, the priests sacrificed two goats on the Day of Atonement, the day once a year on which sacrifices were made for the sins of all Israel. Individual sacrifices were offered regularly throughout the year, but this day was meant for all.

One goat was sacrificed on the altar, its blood sprinkled on the atonement cover within the inner curtain where God dwelt. The other goat—the "scapegoat" or the "goat of removal"—was left alive. The priest placed his hands on the live goat's head and confessed all of the sins of the Israelites, including their sin of rebellion. "Then Aaron shall lay both of his hands on the head of the live goat, and confess over it all the iniquities of the sons of Israel, and all their transgressions in regard to all their sins; and he shall lay them on the head of the goat and send it away into the wilderness . . . " (Lev. 16:21). The goat was then taken and left to wander in the desolate land, to die a slow, agonizing death outside the city walls.

The Old Testament sacrifices served as a type, that is as a picture and foreshadowing, of the true sacrifice to come—Jesus. Not only is Jesus our Lord and Savior, He is also our scapegoat. Not only did he die as atonement for our sins but also as our guilt offering. His was a slow, agonizing death outside the city walls.

When I confessed my sin of premarital sex, like the priest who placed his hands on the goat, I had to spiritually place my hands on the head of Jesus. I transferred my awful sins to Him. He paid for my redemption. He did not just remove my guilt, He took my guilt upon Himself. As He did, He cried, "Father, why have you forsaken Me?" He was forsaken so that I would never be forsaken. Through Jesus' death, I now stand guiltless in His grace.

But forgiveness from sin is sometimes easier to accept than freedom from guilt. *Yes, Lord,* I pray, *I know you forgive me, but I'm not free to love you like brother So-and-So. Brother So-and-So has never done what I did.* Yet to live under the limits of shame after being forgiven is to say that Christ's death atoned for some things but not for others. It is, in essence, to mock the validity of His sacrifice. God's Word says that He offers us the opportunity to repent and to shed our guilt. Take it. If we don't, then we have an even greater sin to confess—the sin of unbelief.

In the old television show, *The Lone Ranger,* a good guy was often tied up and in danger. The Lone Ranger rode in and cut the ropes that held the good guy in bondage, and then they both would ride off in freedom.

Jesus Christ cut the bonds of guilt. Yet, for many years, I remained self-imprisoned. Jesus freed me, but Satan lied to me, telling me that I was still in bondage to guilt. "We come to Christ because of grace," said Teresa, whose premarital sex led to her having an abortion. "But then we deceive ourselves once we get there into believing that grace isn't enough to remove guilt. For a long time, I believed that Jesus forgave sin. But the Devil always whispered, 'Not yours. Not entirely.'"

But we can take comfort from and find truth in Scripture. After David's sin with Bathsheba, he wrote,

> Blessed is he
>   whose transgressions are forgiven,
>   whose sins are covered.
> Blessed is the man
>   whose sin the LORD does not count against him
>   and in whose spirit is no deceit.
>
> When I kept silent,
>   my bones wasted away
>   through my groaning all day long.
> For day and night
>   your hand was heavy upon me;
> my strength was sapped
>   as in the heat of summer.
> Then I acknowledged my sin to you
>   and did not cover up my iniquity.
> I said, "I will confess

> my transgressions to the LORD"—
> and you forgave
> the guilt of my sin.
>
>   —Psalm 32:1–5 NIV

After I repented, I realized that God had also forgiven my guilt. I was beginning to understand what "peace with God" meant and how forgiveness created intimacy. "Look at the story of the woman caught in adultery . . . about to get stoned to death," says youth pastor Bob Bartlett, "and the Son of God picks her up and says, 'No one condemns you, neither do I. Go and sin no more. . . .' Notice that the man she had sex with is nowhere in sight, but here's Jesus forgiving her. . . . Intimacy is connected to forgiveness."[7]

The same forgiveness that God showed me, I now needed to show others. Forgiving, however, wasn't as easy as I had hoped. Satan opposes forgiveness and tries everything to prevent it. "Now if forgiveness is one of the central themes of the Bible—perhaps the central theme," writes Jim Logan, "where do you suppose the enemy might attack you and me as God's children? Through lack of forgiveness. How can I go and tell other men and women the good news that they can be forgiven by God when I am harboring unforgiveness in my own heart?"[8]

By keeping a family bound up in unforgiveness, Satan accomplishes his goal of disarming the body of Christ. I had to realize that my enemy was not Brian. Rather, my enemy was and is Satan. I had to choose to forgive because of the forgiveness given to me. And I had to do so against spiritual opposition. "The enemy lied to me telling me that I could never have a good Christian marriage, that God would not allow it," said Jennifer, a woman who is married to the man with whom she had engaged in premarital sex. "The enemy told me that it would always be like this—with the anger and the fighting."

Satan is the father of lies. He lies to us and tells us that things will not get better. He tells us that our spouses don't deserve our forgiveness. Or he tells us that they will not accept it, or that they haven't changed their behavior and will trample on it. Yet, when we have received God's forgiveness, we must also forgive others. To do less would be disobedient and hypocritical. How could I hold Brian to a higher standard than that to which my Savior held me? It didn't matter whether I felt like forgiving Brian. God said to do it. God said to love one another.

Reclaiming intimacy begins in the mind by choosing to forgive and to love regardless of feelings. Even if one spouse engaged in premarital sex with someone else while the other spouse remained sexually pure until marriage—this doesn't negate the obligation to forgive. I played the adulterous woman in an Easter pageant. Every night, actors threw me down on the stage and hurled angry accusations at me. Then I heard Jesus' words: "He who is without sin cast the first stone." He didn't say those without *sexual* sin could throw the first stone. He said those without *sin*. Some sin happens to be more physically intensive than others, but all sin crucified Jesus.

Were I not to forgive, I would betray Jesus, hurt others, and continue to poison myself against any potential for intimacy. My anger would continue to breed resentment. "Guilt is anger directed at ourselves—at what we did or did not do. Resentment is anger directed at others—at what they did or did not do."[9] Letting go of resentment is a step toward experiencing real intimacy. But how can we do such a difficult thing?

Scripture tells about a young boy named Joseph, who had good reason for resentment. While Joseph relished visions of power and rule, his jealous brothers tried to kill him and then sold him to some slave traders heading to Egypt. Yet there is no record of Joseph displaying a bad attitude over his ordeal. Rather, Scripture records how well Joseph worked as a slave. In fact, he found favor with the wife of one ruler in Egypt, and she tried to seduce him. When he refused her advances, she grew angry and, in her humiliation, accused Joseph of a crime and had him put in prison.

No one would have blamed Joseph if he'd adopted a bad attitude then. Instead, he continued to be close to God while in prison, and this enabled him to interpret the dreams of fellow prisoners. These interpretations led to his early release and his being given a place of power in the Egyptian government.

When famine spread throughout the land of Joseph's brothers, they came to Egypt in search of food. Not recognizing their brother, they bowed before Joseph just as he had seen in his visions when he was a young boy. If Joseph resented his brothers, here was a good opportunity to make them pay. They were at his mercy. But Joseph had forgiven them. He gave them their food, and in the course of time he revealed himself to them and invited the entire family to join him in Egypt. His response should be our response. He said, "Do not be grieved or angry with yourselves" (Gen. 45:5).

While counterfeit intimacy may be rooted in pleasure, authentic intimacy is rooted in God. The Bible doesn't tell women to trust their husbands. Rather, we are told to put our "hope in God" (1 Peter 3:5). Joseph didn't put his trust in people; he put his trust in God. When we trust that God is God over both the wise and unwise decisions that we and others make, we can love our husbands "without being frightened by any fear" (v. 6). We need not fear rejection, being taken advantage of, nonresponsiveness, or loneliness.

Letting go of resentment means trusting that God is God, even of the disappointments in life—the fights, the distance between you and your spouse, any past illicit relationships. It is to believe that "all things . . . work together for *good* to those who love God, to those who are called according to His purpose" (Rom. 8:28, emphasis added). *All things* means even the things we, as well as our spouses, regret. God may use a strained marriage relationship or past failures for His *good* by teaching us to trust Him, obey Him, and draw close to Him.

My relationship with Jesus is marked by love and intimacy beyond any human deserving. I didn't always have that, but now that I do I can't imagine life being worthwhile without it. I didn't turn to Jesus, though, because I was fulfilled in my life. I turned to Him because He allowed me to be empty. I thank God for the stresses that He allowed in my marriage. I am sorry for contributing to those stresses. But without them I would have been tempted to grow passive and become content with a less-than-perfect love. My imperfect marriage, and the results of my misdirected quest, directed my heart to a Perfect Love.

God's ways are higher than our ways and incomprehensible to our understanding. Unless we trust Him, knowing that we will never on this side of eternity understand His ways, we will not feel free to forgive others completely. Yet if we do not forgive others completely, we will not allow vulnerability and intimacy to grow. True intimacy occurs as our trust is redirected from people to God.

If I say, "I desire intimacy," yet I have not repented of premarital sex, I have spoken out of both sides of my mouth. Because the sin itself caused the separation.

If I say, "I desire intimacy," yet continue to harbor resentment against my spouse for his sin of premarital sex, I have spoken out of both sides of my mouth. To forgive him is the right thing to do. God says, "To one who knows the right thing to do, and does not do it, to him it is sin" (James 4:17). My sin has caused the separation.

If I say, "I desire intimacy," yet remain bitter over the physical, emotional, or financial consequences of premarital sex, I have spoken out of both sides of my mouth. Moping over the consequences denies God's rightful sovereignty. My sin, again, has caused the separation.

You may be thinking, *My sin happened over twenty years ago. Why do I need to repent of something I did so long ago and am not doing anymore?* Time doesn't bridge separation. Only Jesus can. Time doesn't make us any closer to God; it only makes us less aware of how far apart from Him we are.

My repentance came some four years after Brian and I had married. It came on a Sunday morning following a sermon about a woman I'd never before heard of. Her name was Gomer, and she was a prostitute. She was taken in marriage by a prophet named Hosea. The Lord had told Hosea to marry Gomer, even though she would be unfaithful to him. The Lord told Hosea, "Go again, love a woman who is loved by her husband, yet an adulteress" (Hos. 3:1). Hosea's covenant with Gomer was based on God's command not on her behavior.

That morning at church I saw God as faithful. Although my behavior did not evoke His love, neither did it provoke Him to abandon me. Rationalizing my sin did not remove me from His covenantal love, nor did it make me more appealing to Him. God was faithful to me when I lacked faith and was utterly undesirable, and He remained so simply because He is faithful. In His faithfulness, I found the freedom to be honest and repent.

I saw that morning that God was holy but that He wouldn't leave me if I told Him what He already knew—that I was not holy. Nor would He love me any less. Rather, however unbelievable to me it seemed, He would delight in my repentance.

I can only say, "Who is a God like Thee, who pardons iniquity and passes over the rebellious act of the remnant of His possession? He does not retain His anger forever, because He delights in unchanging love. He will again have compassion on [me]; He will tread [my] iniquities under foot. Yes, Thou wilt cast all [my] sins into the depths of the sea" (Mic. 7:18–19). After having said . . .

> I repent, making no excuses
> I repent, no one else to blame
> I return to fall in love with Jesus
> I bow down on my knees . . . and I repent . . .[10]

That Sunday morning God drew a circle in red around the cross engraved on my heart. He showed me that the cross is the most important element in my life and in my marriage, and I haven't the slightest desire to wipe the circle away.

8

Trust and Obey

Our family recently made a trip to Tijuana. This was our first time out of the States, and we didn't speak Spanish. To say we were nervous would be an understatement.

The trip had been organized as part of a cross-cultural training course in which we were enrolled. The trip coordinators had provided a map to our hotel, yet we quickly became confused because the street signs were all in Spanish. In no time at all, we were lost. Tijuana is a large city, and for an hour and a half we searched for our hotel. While we could sense the general direction in which to go, we couldn't find a road to take us there.

We eventually gave up trying to get to our hotel and decided to head back toward the border. We could read the signs that said, "USA." We thought we would cross the border, then enter again, and start from scratch. When we got there long lines of cars waited to cross, and we knew it would take at least an hour. Our meeting at the hotel began in fifteen minutes.

So we headed up a narrow road to get out of the long lines. This road, however, brought us face-to-face with Mexican motorcycle police. I guess it was a one-way street, and we were going the wrong way. At least a half dozen Mexican policemen stared at us. I smiled. One of them approached us, and I had visions of a night in jail or a hefty fine. But the policeman smiled back. He didn't speak English, so Brian showed him our map and pointed at our hotel. The policeman chuckled then called another policeman over to our car. The second policeman spoke some English, and he tried giving us directions, but because of our confused expressions he quickly gave up. Then he sighed, turned to his partner, and mumbled something in Spanish. Turning back to us, he said two words: "Follow me." No problem.

We knew the policeman had seen our map, and we had seen the kindness in his eyes. Because we knew he was familiar with the city, we knew we could trust his lead. Obeying him by following him would get us to our hotel, but trusting in him while we obeyed made the journey a joy.

Trusting gave us the freedom to follow without fear. Not once, as we zigzagged in and out of traffic, did we question the policeman's lead. In fact, we no longer even tried to read the street signs. Instead, we joked about our motorcycle escort and how it resembled a scene from *CHIPS*.[1] I got the video camera out and taped our escort. Trusting turned an unnerving experience into a cause for celebration.

To those of us who get lost, Jesus also says, "Follow Me." He has seen the map of our lives, and He is intimately familiar with our world—He not only made it but also lived here. So we know we can trust Him. Following Jesus gets us to where He is leading, but trusting His lead gives us joy along the way. Trust is "confidence in the integrity of another person." Trust is essential to intimacy. Without it, we are not free to experience the joy of loving or being loved.

Reclaiming intimacy in marriage first requires repentance. The next step is trust. But if premarital sex is involved, trust has been violated. If we look only to humans for perfect, trustworthy love, we will end up disillusioned, and intimacy will seem even further out of reach.

We should be leery, too, of self-help formulas that paint rosy pictures of positive relationships based on mutual esteem. To build trust we begin by acknowledging our sins and the limits of our humanity. We are sinners in a sinful world. Jesus didn't *esteem* us when He died for us—He saved us. He didn't validate us—He redeemed us. Jesus loved us enough to die, not because He trusted in our integrity, but because He didn't. That is love. Our intimacy with God is not based on His trust in us. Our intimacy with others should not be based on whether or not they can be trusted to be without sin.

As I drew nearer to God a few years into our marriage, my relationship with Brian also grew closer. I let go of some of the resentment and anger I had toward him and myself, as did Brian. Our arguments occurred less frequently, and our home began to feel like a place of warmth. We spent a great deal of time talking. We went on dates. We bought special things for each other from time to time. For all intents and purposes, our marriage was working.

But we still did things, on occasion, that bothered one another. Perhaps it was an unkind word said in a moment of vulnerability. Maybe it was a change of family plans when something personal came up. Perhaps it was plain inattentiveness. Whatever it was, the actions hurt. When I felt hurt, no matter what the offense, I relived the feelings I experienced in the difficult early days of our marriage. That wasn't fair to Brian.

Although we didn't fight often, when we did I reverted to my behavior in our early days. I returned to what I knew. I said things that weren't nice, as did Brian. My reaction was self-protective—I immediately withdrew from the quest for intimacy and gave up altogether. I would even withdraw from God during those times.

Too many good days and growing experiences were lost while I grieved that my trust had once again been broken. *Would it ever end,* I wondered. *Would Brian ever get it totally together?* He had every reason to wonder the same about me.

During the seventh year of our marriage, after we had been back in church and learning about God for a few years, Brian felt the Lord leading him to attend seminary. *Super,* I thought. *Now he'll finally learn how to be the perfect husband. He'll do all of those things that perfect husbands do.*

After applying to a seminary, Brian left his secure job. With three children—all under the age of six—we moved a million miles away to a foreign place called Texas. I was a stranger in a friendly, but strange land. I no longer had the support structure of both of our families living in the same town, which made it difficult to do anything that required a baby-sitter. We no longer had the secure income of Brian's full-time managerial position. So paying a baby-sitter, could I have found one, was impossible. I also no longer had a home of my own. We ended up renting a lovely but old place that still had previous tenants living behind the walls.

That's okay, I thought. *I have a husband who desires to seek after God and who will undoubtedly, as a result, end up lavishing time and attention on me as he grows. After all, the Bible tells husbands to love their wives. Surely they will teach that one. Besides, how much time can it take to attend some simple seminary classes? Think of all the time we will have together.*

My outlook remained positive as Brian quickly got a part-time job, and as we sprayed the house for bugs. He started those "simple" classes that ended up having massive requirements. He also enjoyed seminary. Enjoyed it? He loved it! He poured his passion into seminary. I, on the other hand, felt neglected and jealous of Old Testament commentaries and even older professors. After three years and a graduation with honors, I still waited for my perfect husband.

Certainly our relationship was deeper and more intimate than in the beginning. We had times of mutual enjoyment when we could grab them. But on occasion Brian made me angry. And okay, on occasion I made him angry as well. During those times we showed our ugly selves and broke trust. All of our difficulties, coupled with the distance between us that resulted from lack of time together, proved incredibly depressing. I despaired that it would ever get any better.

Then, in my anguish, I realized that my love for Brian should be as Jesus' love for me—based, not on trust in a person, but on trust in a perfect God. God is the perfect Husband whose love can fill the greatest need. So in order to love, as does Jesus, without expecting to be loved in return, I needed to place *my* need for love with my Beloved. Then, whatever happened, be it a hurtful exchange or just plain complacency, I would know that I was still loved. Pain would only push me to my "Totally Other," whom I could trust. If I trusted God completely, I would be acknowledging the truth that nothing would ever hurt me that He had not first approved for *good*.

My seven-year-old daughter recently came to me with a new thought on God. She said, "Mom, guess what? God is a box." I waited. She went on, "God is a box, and I am inside the box. Nothing can get to me without first having to go through God, the box."

The wisdom of children. No one can hurt me, disappoint me, or break my trust without first being allowed to do so by God. His sovereign hand is upon me, and His limitless knowledge goes before me. Even the pain I experience from my sin or from other people's sin must first pass through the box of God's protection and sovereignty.

"You must learn to love other people without expecting any friendship from them at all," writes Fenelon. "People tend to be quite fickle. They love us and leave us, they go and come. They shift from one position to another like a kite in the wind, or like a feather in the breeze. Let them do as they will. Just be sure that you see only God in them. They could do nothing to you without His permission. So, in the end, it is He that tests or blesses us, using them as you have need."[2]

God says that *all* things work together for good to those who love Him. Yet Satan would have me believe that I can't trust God. That thought was at the very root of his lie to Eve. The serpent said, "Did God *really* say . . . ?" Satan tries to discount what God says by using circumstances in our lives. God's greatest commandment is to love. If we were to obey Him, we would have intimacy overflowing. But Satan lies to us to get us to question God. Satan asks, "Did God really say . . . love? Even when someone isn't nice to you? Even when someone has had premarital sex with you, and you have dishonored each other? Even when someone lacks integrity or is aloof? Did God *really* say . . . love?"

It is only to the level that we trust in God's goodness, thus disarming the lie, that we can be truly intimate with others. When we trust God as we follow Him, we can experience joy on the way by loving freely. Yet trust does not mean abandonment to naïveté. A person with a history of sexual immorality, even to a small degree, may prove a greater risk for sexual sin in the future. He or she may be cynical and unfeeling so as to camouflage tender emotions.

It is not good for a drug addict to hang out with people who are smoking pot. Nor should an alcoholic spend weekends in a bar. People with sexual pasts need to recognize, or at least they need to ask themselves, to what extent they are sensitive to temptation in the areas of sexuality and emotional suppression. "Because we have had sexual pasts," says Cheryl, "my husband and I have made a conscious effort to be very cautious of what we expose ourselves to. We are cautious of what movies we see, who we are around, and what we let into our minds." This couple has evaluated their weaknesses and taken steps to avoid risk.

Transferring trust from others to God, though, does not mean to *dis*trust people. Rather it means trusting a person through the wisdom of the One who knows what's best. The book of Hosea illustrates a trust in God that results in fellowship and intimacy. As has been already seen, the Lord had instructed his prophet Hosea to marry the prostitute Gomer and have children by her. When Hosea's family was established, his wife committed adultery again. But the Lord told him, "Love her as the LORD loves the Israelites, though they turn to other gods" (Hos. 3:1 NIV). How exactly did the Lord love the Israelites?

Following the above passage, the next ten chapters of Hosea lament Israel's idolatry and sinfulness. Reading through these condemnations, one wonders how God would ever have anything to do with these people again, let alone trust them. Yet in the final chapter of Hosea, God offers a call to repentance to Israel:

> Return, O Israel, to the LORD your God,
> For you have stumbled because of your iniquity.
> Take words with you and return to the LORD.
> Say to Him, "Take away all iniquity,
> And receive us graciously,
> That we may present the fruit of our lips.
> Assyria will not save us,
> We will not ride on horses;
> Nor will we say again, 'Our god,'
> To the work of our hands;
> For in Thee the orphan finds mercy."
>
> —Hosea 14:1–3

In essence, God has directed them to repent of pride and pleasure, and step into the presence of a holy God. In response to their
repentance, the Lord promises, "I will heal their apostasy, I will
love them freely" (14:4, emphasis added).

The Lord has promised to love Israel freely—that is, unconditionally. Knowing Israel's past, it is difficult to understand how He
could. It is possible only with His love, which is rooted in His
faithfulness, not in human trustworthiness. Theologian J. I. Packer
writes,

> It is staggering that God should love sinners; yet it is true.
> God loves creatures who have become unlovely and (one
> would have thought) unlovable. There was nothing what-
> ever in the objects of his love to call it forth . . . nothing in us
> could attract or prompt it. Love among persons is awak-
> ened by something in the beloved, but the love of God is
> free, spontaneous, unevoked, uncaused. God loves people
> because he has chosen to love them . . . and no reason for his
> love can be given except his own sovereign good pleasure.[3]

Consider what God speaks through Hosea concerning Israel's
return: "'In that day,' declares the LORD, 'you will call me "my
husband"; you will no longer call me "my master." ' . . . I will betroth you in righteousness and justice, in love and compassion. I
will betroth you in faithfulness, and you will acknowledge the
LORD'" (Hos. 2:16, 19–20 NIV).

Some translations choose the word "chain" rather than "betroth,"
as in a wedding. Both words illustrate the concept of covenant.
God "chains" us to Him in His righteousness, justice, love, and
compassion. How can He trust us enough to "love us freely?" Because as children of God, we are chained in His faithfulness and
His faithfulness is trustworthy. God can trust Himself.

Will we still sin? Yes. But Christ has made the atonement. Will we still hurt each other, even during very intimate stages of our marriages? Yes. Like Brian and I in Tijuana, we are all foreigners to righteousness. We try to follow the map God has set before us, but we get lost. On the quest for authentic intimacy, we will sometimes head the wrong way on a one-way street. But Jesus will meet us there and say, "Follow Me." It will be up to us to follow. If we follow Him, trusting in His lead, He will escort us toward intimacy.

Brian will tell you that I am not a perfect mate. But we both have met Someone who is. Because of His perfection, we know we can freely trust Him. Through Him, we have found the freedom to trust one another, as well.

9

I Want to Fall in
Love with You

A woman took a stroll down a country lane. Coming upon a neighboring farm, she noticed the farmer held a crossbow.

"What's going on, Farmer Tom?" she asked.

"I'm taking up archery," he said.

The woman looked at the barn where Tom had aimed. Every arrow rested right in the center of a bull's-eye! "That's some fine shooting, Farmer Tom," the woman said and continued on her way.

"Thanks," responded the farmer, taking aim and letting another arrow fly.

Glancing over her shoulder, the woman saw the arrow hit the barn. But this one didn't hit a target; it just hit the barn. Then she saw Farmer Tom stroll over to the barn, pick up his paint bucket and brush, and paint a circle around the arrow.

All along, Farmer Tom hadn't been aiming for any bull's-eyes. He thought hitting the side of the barn was good enough. It only took a couple of strokes of paint to make it look like his arrows had hit the target.

When I engaged in premarital sex, I became like Farmer Tom. I didn't aim at authentic intimacy but shot in the general direction of what looked like love and thought that would be good enough. I could always paint a bull's-eye later to give the illusion that I'd struck true intimacy.

Once married, I aimed at escaping loneliness and thought painting the bull's-eye around my arrows would make me feel secure. The tendency I had refined while engaging in premarital sex, that of aiming at people to feel fulfilled, continued. Seeking to satisfy the longings of my heart through people had grown into a habit.

When I got married, I aimed at things to fulfill me, and I painted bull's-eyes around what I'd hit—a nice home, children, and church involvement with Brian. With my arrows in so many bull's-eyes, I was surrounded by illusions of hitting actual intimacy.

I had relied on premarital sex to make me feel that I had an intimate relationship with Brian. But when arguments, trials, and emotional detachment came between us, I no longer had premarital sex to fall back on. I saw it for the lie it really was.

Even so, I was used to looking for the validation, or expression, of intimacy in tangible areas of my flesh. I turned, then, to new things in my relationship with Brian to confirm our affection for each other. They, too, didn't last—especially past the next fight or during times of mutual dissatisfaction. After many years of this, I realized that I had been looking to Brian to meet a need within me that he was not even capable of meeting. Gary Thomas explains it this way in his book *Sacred Marriage:*

> We need to remind ourselves of the ridiculousness of look-ing for something from other humans that only God can provide. Our close friends have a son named Nolan. When he was just four years old, he saw me carrying some rather large boxes and asked me, in all sincerity, "Gary, are you strongest, or is God strongest?"

His dad laughed a little too hard at that one. And of course we adults think it's absurd to compare our physical strength with God's. But how many of us "adults" have then turned around and asked, perhaps unconsciously, "Are you going to fulfill me, or will God fulfill me?" For some reason, that question doesn't sound as absurd to us as the one about physical strength, but it should! . . . My wife can't be God, and I was created with a spirit that craves God. Anything less than God, and I'll feel an ache.[1]

To reclaim authentic intimacy that has been lost to disillusionment, dishonor, or disappointment through the sin of premarital sex, we must stop aiming at humans altogether and aim at where real intimacy is found—in Jesus. We succeed in hitting the bull's-eye through what has already been discussed—repentance and trust. We also hit the target through pursuit. We must aim the arrows at the Author of intimacy Himself. Then let go.

Reclaiming intimacy involves dying to self, pursuing holiness, and modeling the love of Jesus.

Dying to Self

When God chose to be intimate with us, He chose to be intimate with a people who are lost (Luke 19:10), perishing (John 3:16), and condemned (v. 18). God gave His perfect love to lovers of darkness and evil (v. 20). He poured His absolute grace on us— we who are lulled to sleep in the lap of the Evil One (1 John 5:19), are formed in iniquity (Ps. 51:5), and are desperately wicked (Jer. 17:9). God loved the unlovable.

In order for a holy God to be intimate with us, a sacrifice just as holy had to be made. Jesus was that sacrifice. He hung on a cross for the sins of the whole world. He painted a picture of true love framed in service, self-sacrifice, and death. "He humbled Himself by becoming obedient to the point of death, even death on a cross" (Phil. 2:8). Jesus died to Himself in every sense of the term.

To die to ourselves means giving up our hopes, our dreams, and our aspirations in order to follow Jesus. It means laying our self-will, our pride, and our need to control on the altar and letting them die as a sacrifice. It means loving our spouses because God says to love, even if thoughts of our spouses' past relationships haunt us. Paul basically stated it this way: We ought to consider others as more important than ourselves (see Rom. 12:10). We can't do that unless we first learn to die to ourselves.

But the struggles of everyday life grab my attention more than the pursuit of dying to self. I find myself too often responding to the small, everyday irritations in the same way I approached pre-marital sex—selfishly.

Let's say Brian says he'll take over the household chores for a few days so that I can get some things done. Great! After two days the dishwasher is begging to be loaded. *It's not my turn,* I think. *He said he would take care of everything.* So the dishwasher remains empty. Or I find a stray pair of Brian's shoes in the hallway, and I leave them there because the owner is old enough to put them away.

Or maybe I am in a social situation. The conversation gets turned toward me. Do I relish the attention, or do I change the focus to Brian so as to honor him? Too many times I enjoy my conceit rather than practicing the humility that comes from exalting another through praise.

Premarital sex didn't make me this way, but it did cultivate my selfishness. In order to cultivate dying to self I need the virtue of grace. Even though I have been forgiven my sin of premarital sex, my flesh remains trained in the habit that premarital sex encouraged—feeding myself. In order to die to myself, I have to acknowledge my innate self-interest and change my thinking.

Whoever engages in premarital sex feeds his or her flesh, thus creating a barrier to reclaiming intimacy. Feeding the flesh the tasty morsels of selfishness only increases a desire for self-gratification. Instead of prayers steeped in humility, we may find ourselves praying, "Give me a husband who understands that I have other responsibilities besides him," or "Give me a wife who understands all I have to accomplish and go through at work," or "Give me a spouse who understands and cares for everything I think. Everything I say. Everything I feel." Give me! Give me! Give me!

Me. We have painted ourselves—our own expectations and desires—around the arrows. We've made ourselves the bull's-eye when aiming at authentic intimacy, thus revealing that premarital sex is nothing more than a manifestation of our own selfishness. We need to be honest, to name it and claim it for what it is and for what it has done—fostered even more selfishness. Only by recognizing what premarital sex really is and what has resulted from it can we change our hearts and minds. Dr. Larry Crabb writes,

> Only when the central problem of self-centeredness is faced first and squarely can a *desire* to do right develop. . . . Married folks would do well to think *less* about doing what good husbands and wives should do or whether they are properly taking their humanness into account, and *more* about how self-directed so much of their activity really is. Rather than figuring out practical ways to improve our marriages, perhaps we need to realize how badly and how often we need forgiveness. . . . We want manageable activity and practical handles to guide us through the confusing times in our lives. But we will not be able to take the positive steps toward the enjoyment marriage was designed to provide until we first take steps to recognize more clearly the selfishness we so easily excuse.[2]

Neither will we be able to reclaim intimacy until we first realize that, when seeking intimacy, the one on whom we focus is usually ourselves. To reclaim intimacy, our focus must be redirected from ourselves to God. Because of the mercies of God, we ought to aim our arrows for heaven.

Paul writes, "You were raised from the dead with Christ. So *aim at what is in heaven,* where Christ is sitting at the right hand of God. Think only about the things in heaven, not the things on earth. Your old sinful self *has died,* and your new life is kept with Christ in God. Christ is your life" (Col. 3:1–4 NCV, emphasis added).

Dying to self means living to Christ. Jesus taught us how to aim at heaven when He taught us to pray, "Thy kingdom come. Thy will be done, on earth as it is in heaven" (Matt. 6:10). Asking for God's will to be done on earth as it is in heaven, is requesting a bit of heaven to exist down here. We thereby acknowledge the fullness of God in heaven, His attributes and environment. We are saying, "I want a little of what You've got in heaven. I want what You want. I want Your will in heaven to be done here where I am. I want You! I want to fall in love with You!"

More likely, though, we find ourselves praying, "My kingdom come. My will be done." Doing so only paints bull's-eyes around our own selfish desires and creates an illusion of intimacy. We thus miss the target of intimacy altogether, settling for merely hitting the side of a barn.

Jesus died to His own will so that the unloving could love. We are to follow His example and die to self—in order to live. "Truly, truly, I say to you, unless a grain of wheat falls into the earth and dies, it remains by itself alone; but if it dies, it bears much fruit. He who loves his life loses it; and he who hates his life in this world shall keep it to life eternal" (John 12:24–25).

Dying to self means dying to earthly expectations. It means

embracing true humility. Humility cannot be offended because it demands nothing. "It is in the death to self that humility is perfected," writes Andrew Murray.

> Be sure that at the root of all real experience of more grace, or all true advance in consecration, of all actually increasing conformity to the likeness of Jesus, there must be a deadness to self that proves itself to God and men in our dispositions and habits. . . . The death to self has no surer death mark than a humility which makes itself of no reputation, which empties out itself, and takes the form of a servant.[3]

Reclaiming intimacy includes dying to self that is then manifested outwardly in acts of service, forgiveness, and honor.

Marriage is not a place to practice complacency. It is one of the most difficult institutions ever created. It requires the molding of two incomplete people who have a notion that satisfying their wants and desires is the aim of their lives. Unless this notion is got rid of, and got rid of quickly through dying to self, the marriage will become a competition for control and a wasteland of selfishness.

"If people understood the depth of self-abnegation that marriage demands, there would perhaps be far fewer weddings," writes Mike Mason. "For marriage, too, would be seen as a form of suicide. It would not be seen as a way of augmenting one's comfort and security in life, but rather as a way of losing one's life for the sake of Christ."[4]

Pursuing Holiness

Dying to self means living for Jesus. It means resting in Jesus—recognizing and relying on what He wants. Living for Jesus can mean only one kind of life—a life of holiness. While forgiveness for our sin of premarital sex came freely upon repentance, personal holiness in the quest for intimacy comes with a cost. Victory to overcome what sin has created—increased selfishness, skepticism, and relational vices—requires effort and a daily resting in Jesus.

"You can become a Christian for free but it is expensive to be a disciple," says Dr. Tony Evans. "You can go to heaven for free but to get heaven to come down here and join you on earth costs something. . . . What's the difference between a victorious marriage and a defeated marriage? Discipleship."[5]

Discipleship is the learning of and adapting to the teachings of Jesus. One way we can learn about Jesus is by looking at His life. Jesus' life reveals virtues of gentleness, humility, service, grace, power, and compassion. Numerous books have been written on how to cultivate these virtues.[6] But time alone with God and in His Word is the best way to gain understanding of His teachings. His Word is the only thing that hasn't been tainted by human ambition or fear. It is the only thing that can displace the lies that the Enemy has birthed through sins such as premarital sex.

In her book *Praying God's Word,* Beth Moore sorts Scripture into prayers that we can use to shield our minds against the Enemy's lies.[7] Sections of the book contain prayers that are relevant to challenges resulting from premarital sex, challenges such as overcoming pride, idolatry, sexual strongholds, and the insecurity of feeling unloved. It is a palatable resource for renewing the mind.

In praying God's Word, we not only battle against the enemy but also we battle our flesh to purify our thoughts. The process of resting in the Holy One begins with renewing our minds with Truth.

Then, when we try to apply and carry out the truth of Jesus daily in our own lives, we enter a process of becoming holy. Holiness simply means set apart and different. In spiritual holiness, we are set apart from sin and the flesh. We become different from our own natures.

My nature, for example, says to think of my wants first. Holiness says to think first of others. My nature says to hold back physical affection at the times when I regret how easily I gave it before I was married. Holiness says to forgive and give generously. My nature tells me to ignore efforts to make myself physically appealing to my spouse when I believe Satan's lie that I was sought prior to marriage solely on the basis of the physical. Holiness says to honor my husband, and one way I can honor him is through his desire for physical appeal.

Holiness means that we are to become different from our natures, which have nursed us and comforted us. Our perception of holiness may be intimidating or fuzzy at first. But in time our minds will be renewed with the Truth, which gives us clear perception and a reflection of God's glory.

And that vision may, at first, be overwhelming. Annie Dillard, in her book *Pilgrim at Tinker Creek*, tells about an incident that took place in the early 1900s when surgeons in the West perfected cataract surgery. These surgeons traveled extensively, performing the operation and giving sight to people who had been blind from cataracts, some since birth. Many of the adult patients became horrified after the procedure. Some, in fact, chose to return to blindness by closing their eyes and keeping them closed. Because their brains were at first unable to distinguish space, depth, and size, the patients could not associate meaning to what they saw. They were unable to decipher walls, which they bumped into, or a shoe over which they would trip. Shadows looked like objects that had to be reckoned with.

Their experience is similar to the blind man whom Jesus healed. Upon restoration of his sight, the man interpreted people as trees that walked. Jesus then placed His hands on the blind man's eyes a second time and performed another miracle—that of creating perception for the man as well.

The surgeons in Dillard's book couldn't create perception for their patients. Instead, the patients had to go through the daunting process of learning it on their own. Before the operation, many of the patients were happy, oblivious to the reality around them. After the operation, many of them were stressed with an overload of perceptions. Having been given new sight, some preferred to return to darkness instead.

Sight was foreign to these patients, as holiness is foreign to all of us. It goes against our flesh. It is in opposition to our natures. We can become so overwhelmed when we read God's Word and see Jesus' holiness that we prefer to close our eyes and remain in darkness. We prefer to remain in the abstract world of touching rather than risk being overwhelmed by the details of actually seeing. We close our eyes, finding it difficult to focus on anything at all except what we can feel—our flesh.

Our spirits have not been trained to distinguish the depths and shapes of true holiness. The initial perception frightens us. Yet through time and practice, like a cataract patient whose eyes focus more clearly each day, we will see and become what God has intended. And in His holiness, we will learn how to reclaim intimacy that is lasting.

Although the pursuit of holiness can be overwhelming, it must nonetheless be done on an individual basis. Pursuing holiness through Jesus might be compared to a football game. Everyone in the stadium gets to experience the game—but at different levels of involvement. A sizeable difference exists between the satisfaction found by those who sit in the nosebleed seats versus those in the first row on the fifty-yard line. An even greater difference in experiencing the game exists between spectator and player.

All Christians are able to pursue holiness through Jesus. But not all Christians climb onto the field to do so. Some are content to remain in the stands as spectators. Without making a willful choice to play the game and go against the opposition—Satan and our own flesh—it is impossible to score and thereby attain intimacy.

When Brian used to play football, the quarterback would hand him the ball and Brian would run toward the goal line. In all of the games I saw, Brian always scored because every time he got the ball he dashed for the goal.

As a pom-pom girl, I often sat in the front row of the bleachers, cheering him on. Yet no matter how much Brian liked me, never once did he run to me when he got the ball. In fact, he never even looked my way. Had he done so, he wouldn't have scored. And the coach would have sidelined him for sure.

Football players know where the goal is. They know that the goal isn't in the bleachers. It isn't in the band corral. It isn't even at the nacho stand. The moment they start believing it is, they lose the game. What if Brian had said, "But Coach, I get weak in the knees for nachos. I can smell the melted cheese with chili peppers. When I get the ball, all I can think about are nachos, and I just have to go get some."

His coach would have replied, "Then don't play football. Get in the stands with the rest of the spectators! Eat your nachos. Feed your flesh. But don't expect to reach the goal."

The intimacy that was lost in my marriage, resulting from my sin of premarital sex, wasn't going to be reclaimed by watching others pursue holiness. If I wanted to reclaim intimacy through pursuing holiness I was going to have to get out of the stands filled with all of the appeals to the flesh and get on the playing field. If I wanted to reclaim marital intimacy with Brian, I had to learn that the authentic intimacy I innately desired would be found only after much effort and conscious pursuit.

No one else can pursue holiness for me. No one else can attain intimacy for me. I can't even rely on Brian to grow and give me total intimacy. I have to get beyond the distractions and fears of life and focus on pursuing holiness myself. I not only have to focus on it, but I have to actually participate in it. Achieving holiness is not a spectator sport. I have to spend time alone with God in meditation and prayer. I have to read books written about the pursuit of holiness. I have to seek accountability for growth and participate in Bible studies. I have to practice the virtues that I am learning. I have to learn that, while no one can do it for me, neither can I do it on my own. My pursuit may be individual, but it is only done by resting in another individual—Jesus.

When I rest in Jesus, He does the striving for me. And in His striving, I find peace. Brian knows when I am resting in Jesus. He says he can feel a huge weight lift from his shoulders. He can then be free to be himself, because I am not looking to him to meet all of my needs. Rather I am looking to Jesus. In Jesus, my needs are met. And I'll tell you a secret. When a husband feels free to be himself, he usually also feels free to be more kind, gentle, and loving.

Those virtues are a reflection of God's glory here on earth and clearly reflect the pursuit of holiness. In heaven we will, of course, embody perfect holiness. If we want to pursue a life of holiness in Jesus, we will need to aim our hearts toward heaven. By looking at how we will be in heaven, we can understand a little bit what heaven on earth—that is, holiness—looks like. The apostle Paul wrote, "For our citizenship is in heaven, from which also we eagerly wait for a Savior, the Lord Jesus Christ; who will transform the body of our humble state into conformity with the body of His glory" (Phil. 3:20–21).

In this passage is a glimpse of what it means to be in heaven. God's will in heaven includes our bodies being transformed into conformity with the body of His glory. He didn't say the body of *our* glory. Rather, He said we will be transformed into a body that conforms to the glory of Jesus Christ. In heaven we will be reflecting God's glory.

In Isaiah, it says that the whole earth is already "full of [God's] glory" (6:3). If the earth—made up of sinful creatures and a creation groaning for eternity—is full of God's glory, then heaven—a sinless and perfect place—must be overflowing. Imagine the earth as a bottle of soda. We sip from it and enjoy the wonderful tastes and smells. Heaven, however, is like a bottle of soda that has been shaken up. Pop the cap and stand back. God's glory shoots out and floods us in a continuous cascade.

In our pursuit of holiness, lest we get tempted toward prideful thoughts, we must remember that God's glory exists intrinsically within Him. Every ounce of God's glory has already been determined by His character and displayed through His creation. We can add nothing to God's glory. He is the King of Kings and Lord of Lords, larger than the universe and perfect in power—without our help. Yet, through His Son, we have the awesome privilege of reflecting His glory to others. A reflection reveals only an image of something that already exists.

When Moses descended from Mount Sinai, after having seen God's "hind parts" in passing, his face reflected God's glory. Moses didn't determine how much of God's glory he wanted to reflect; rather his face shone as a result of having experienced it.

I can't say, "God, I want about seven dollar's worth of your glory today, please," then expect to live a holy life. Neither can I say, "I'll do this, this, and such-and-such, but no more." Does a mirror dictate to a person how much of that person's image it will reflect? Holiness is emptying one's entire self before an all-consuming and holy God. The reflection, then, is His doing, and it is beautiful.

To reclaim intimacy in my marriage, I had to die to my selfish desires and to myself. I had to redirect my attention from myself to Jesus. I had to fall in love with Him—I should say that I *got* to fall in love with Him. When I did, I wanted to live a life that would be pleasing to Him—a life of holiness. I wanted to be discipled and to emulate Him. Although the initial perception of holiness overwhelmed me, I continued pursuing it, knowing I could not rely on others to do it for me. I took up the never-ending pursuit of holiness, not by striving toward it, but in resting in the Holy One. As I have discovered this new life in Jesus, the intimacy I have gained with Brian has become priceless. It is a peaceful, mysterious, and secure intimacy because it is a reflection of the unchanging and inexplicable glory of God.

Modeling the Love of Jesus

Aiming our quest for intimacy toward heaven is, of course, more difficult than aiming it at the side of a barn. Aiming for heaven means hitting a small cross from quite a distance. It means modeling my life after Jesus. Looking to Jesus as the way to reclaim intimacy in my marriage meant I had to stop thinking about what I wanted to get out of my relationship. I had to learn to love as Jesus loved, serve as Jesus served, and give as Jesus gave. Beyond learning how to do these things, I actually needed to do them. *That's the tough part.*

While washing the disciples' feet, Jesus told them that the blessing was in the doing, not in knowing why it must be done. In washing the disciples' feet, Jesus illustrated love, service, and giving through action.

An awareness of heaven and the virtues of Jesus will do little for reclaiming intimacy unless it is accompanied by action. I'm thankful our Lord wasn't content with just knowing that we are sinners needing to be saved and knowing that He is our perfect salvation. I'm grateful He went ahead and did something about it. His knowledge didn't save me. His death did.

It was late, and Brian and I had been driving all day. We cruised down the interstate in Little Red, our car, at sixty-five miles-per-hour. I had brought a book with me about how to be a helpful wife and was underlining important parts. The car suddenly hit a series of bumps then skidded to a halt just short of a ditch. I looked up from my book and saw that we had stopped in the median at a Y in the interstate.

I asked Brian, "Why did you stop?"

"I came to a split in the road," he said, "and I didn't know which way to go."

I was in charge of reading the map, and I had known that a split in the interstate was coming up. I had simply forgotten to keep my eye open for it or to warn Brian. At that moment, I had been more preoccupied with reading about how to be a helpful wife than with actually being one.

Knowledge apart from action may lead to bumps in any relationship. Some of the actions we see Jesus modeling for us include unconditional love, sacrificial service, and giving in grace.

Unconditional love means I do not love based on what I might receive in return or on the performance of my spouse. Jesus loved his disciples while they doubted him and betrayed him. He loved them even as they grew complacent and, while He was in need, fell asleep instead of praying with Him.

Jesus shows us relational love that does not keep score. He didn't withhold love from Peter as Peter began to sink when he took his eyes off Him. Instead, Jesus lifted Peter from the water. Jesus didn't withhold love from Peter even after Peter denied three times that he knew Jesus.

Unconditional love means reaching out and fostering intimacy even when no intimacy is returned. It means acting in love toward others as they wrestle with their own processes of growth.

Some time ago I had been grumpy for a few days, which usually changes the atmosphere in the house. But Brian refused to be baited. He kept showing kindness, even going out of his way to do so. I grew irritated with him for being so nice in spite of me and asked him what was up. He said with a smile, "I've determined to show you unconditional love, especially when you are grumpy." My grumpiness went away, melted by kindness.

Sacrificial service means service that costs something and is given without recognition. Reclaiming intimacy means also reclaiming honor. Honor is shown through acts of service and esteeming another higher than oneself. I must graciously fulfill responsibilities that benefit my spouse without expectation of anything in return. That is true honor.

I'm a stickler for cooking practical meals. I find no sense in spending hours of preparation on something that will be consumed in a matter of minutes. So my meals often lack the aesthetic value that comes with an extra touch. But I know that Brian appreciates a nice table filled with delicious foods made from scratch with everything beautifully and colorfully arranged. He enjoys cooking and creating such meals, but he enjoys even more being the beneficiary of someone else's hard work.

To Brian, a table filled with a variety of carefully prepared dishes says "I love you" better than my words ever could. I don't do the Chef Heather thing as much as I should, but I do it more than I used to. And I will continue trying to cultivate intimacy through expressions of service. I've got plans today to make Brian's favorite pie—vanilla cream—from scratch. I can't wait to see his smile.

Although sacrificial service is meant to be performed without expectations, it may sometimes be reciprocated. One evening, after I had prepared a very nice meal and served it with extra attention to making our home, children, and me pleasing to him, Brian shooed me out the door. He said, "I'll do the dishes and put the kids to bed. You go shopping and buy that ring you've had your eye on." The ring wasn't a reward. It was his way of expressing the love that sacrificial service had aroused within him.

Jesus served and honored us with His death on the cross, knowing that we could never repay or, in our earthly state, even adequately acknowledge His action. He served us to glorify God. Jesus tells us to do all things as to the Lord. When we serve and honor others, we render our service ultimately to God. We can do it without fear and with a whole heart, because God is worthy of all honor.

Giving in grace means choosing to give continually. Giving cannot vary with moods, which can fluctuate with memories associated with premarital sexual experiences. Giving in grace is never biased.

Stacey, for example, was motivated to have premarital sex as a way of feeling accepted and valuable. The fleshly reason she engaged in premarital sex will not cease to exist simply because she has now married. Her views on the purpose of sex simply present themselves now on the marriage bed. Over time, Stacey's husband may be able to predict a pattern in her advances. Sex usually accompanies days when Stacy has low self-esteem or feels rejection in any area of her life. When Stacey's husband recognizes this pattern, he may be emotionally less intimate during sexual relations because he senses that he is not the object of affection but rather a means to an end.

Yet giving in grace means offering complete emotion and vulnerability, even in the awareness that feelings are not being reciprocated. Rather than withdrawing, it means giving of oneself totally, because through giving, the legitimate needs of the other are honored. Giving of oneself truly and in an honest way through sexual relations can only be done in the absence of anger and doubt. That can happen only when grace to give is present.

But who possesses the ability to love unconditionally through service and giving? Not me. And not you. It is only He who is perfect in all ways. "I can do all things through [Christ] who strengthens me" (Phil. 4:13). And He can do all things through me if I rest in Him. I cannot expect to find the strength and love of Jesus in my marriage if I do not first daily pursue His strength and love, if I do not daily live in His strength and love.

To reclaim intimacy meant I had to stop aiming my quest for intimacy at human beings and aim it instead at God. "If you want to get warm you must stand near the fire," writes C. S. Lewis. "If you want to be wet you must get into the water. If you want joy, power, peace . . . you must get close to, or even into, the thing that has them."[8]

If you want intimacy, you must aim at the One who embodies it—Jesus. Take your eyes off the counterfeit bull's-eyes of your own desires and set them on Him. Imitate Him with others. Emulate Him to others. Adore Him for yourself. When you do, you will soon find that those bull's-eyes you painted "grow strangely dim in the light of His glory and grace." You will also find that reclaiming intimacy in your marriage is not only possible—it is natural. You only need to aim at the right target.

10

Finding My Way

Here are some things that people from varying age groups have learned over the course of their lives, which I received as an e-mail message. A six-year-old girl learned that her dog doesn't want to eat her broccoli either. A twenty-seven year old woman learned that wherever she goes, the world's worst drivers have followed her there. A thirty-eight-year-old woman learned that there are people who love you dearly but just don't know how to show it.

Reclaiming intimacy includes learning how to show love.

Brian and I had been married six years, and we had begun to resolve many of the problems and regrets that had resulted in arguments. We had done so through more than a thousand hours of talking together alone and by turning our hearts toward God and then to each other. I was actively involved in a women's Bible study, and Brian was being discipled via the radio sermons of David Jeremiah and the late J. Vernon McGee.

It was my birthday, and I had gone to bed. Brian's management position kept him late at the store. I woke when I felt something move my hand. Brian had taken my wedding ring off my finger and slipped a new one on in its place. He smiled and kissed me.

There was nothing wrong with my original wedding ring, but Brian knew that I had regretted not having time to look for just the right one. Because of our hasty wedding plans, my ring had been chosen based on availability and price. Honestly, I never liked it. Brian thought that my birthday would be a great time to give me a gift I would cherish. He showed his love by giving me a new ring that I loved and desired.

Saying you love someone and showing you love someone are two different things. Years later, after Brian had graduated from seminary, we were on a pretty tight budget. In one of our long talks he had learned how special flowers are to me. Every week, month after month, Brian would bring me a beautiful bouquet of flowers. And every week, we would spend cherished time together on a date "even if it means we end up in the poor house," he would say. We didn't end up in the poor house, but we did end up in a home filled with love—and vanilla cream pies.

Building intimacy requires a number of things, but at its core it is the knitting of two hearts into one. In this case, one plus one really does equal one. And creating that equation requires depths of disclosure, vulnerability, and openness. "Marriage is about nakedness, exposure, defenselessness, and the very extremities of intimacy," writes Mike Mason. "It is about simple unadorned truth between two human beings. . . . The very heart of intimacy is reached when two people are neither afraid nor ashamed of being possessed by love, when in fact they give themselves freely to the pure joy and liberty of owning and being owned."[1]

The ring Brian placed on my finger delighted me with its beauty. But it enchanted me even more with its meaning. My new ring wasn't a second thought in an uncomfortable situation. It was a carefully chosen symbol of commitment and worth, signifying deep devotion. Intimacy means being willing to be devoted and risking all, because two people giving their all is the hallmark of becoming one. Brian knew I would never be the perfect wife when he gave me the new ring. Intimacy ignores standards and embraces unity. In a letter he wrote to me around that time, he said, "My dearest Heather, I fully commit to receive you because of the sovereignty of God that directed you to me no matter what the circumstances. I commit to you that I will learn to love your differences and weaknesses because they are the things that God gave you to make our relationship whole."

A relationship that is whole acknowledges the need for people to join together. Unity takes broken strands and intertwines them into one whole. Intimacy is never about becoming perfect—it is about becoming one.

My fears sometimes overshadow my efforts to help myself. But when I share my scariest thoughts with my husband, and he points me to God to overcome them, I become whole. Brian is able to help me, because he knows me. He knows what I need to hear, and if he doesn't know exactly, he knows the One to direct me to.

When we acknowledge need, we reveal a dependence that, once revealed, is irrevocable. Intimacy is created when two people acknowledge their needs in the anticipation that each will, with the grace of giving, meet that need for the other. Only when the anticipation is sweet will human nature, which is innately self-protective, venture exposure. But, oh, the return to a heart laid bare when it meets the one chosen by God to reflect His love and affections.

Recently I was flipping through a marriage workbook I had received several years ago. Brian and I each got one when we attended a marriage enrichment conference. A section in the book provides space to write down the different things you want to talk about later with your spouse. Apparently, when I wasn't looking Brian swiped my notebook and wrote under *needs,* "I need you, Heather!" It was a simple acknowledgment but deeply felt. We hadn't gone to the conference because things were tough. It was more of a getaway weekend. Brian's words were an affirmation as well as a revelation.

How often do we tell each other our needs? Couples may often tell each other what they perceive as needs—take out the garbage, pick up the laundry. But how often does one spouse take the other by the hand and relate the genuine needs of his or her soul? Do we stop ourselves from doing this because we are afraid of being corrected? *You shouldn't need more affirmation; it only leads to pride.* Or, *You don't need sex more often; you need to learn patience.* Enough instances of being corrected, and we may take our needs elsewhere.

Yet for a marriage to reclaim intimacy, both partners must embrace risk. Risk lays all the cards on the table to be seen by one's playmate in life. If the response isn't what we desire, our natural tendency is to withdraw or retaliate. But sincere love remains vulnerable. "It takes a wise person to have the last word . . . and not use it." Often, love is demonstrated through restraint. Disappointment must be controlled or it will control.

A lack of restraint during times of disappointment or anger can dampen the intimacy in a marriage by dissolving the safe environment necessary for continued vulnerability. Below are some suggestions for keeping communication open during times of tension:

- *Proactive talking.* This is time set aside weekly or biweekly solely for the purpose of discussing expectations about roles and the relationship.
- *Following fair-fighting rules.* These rules may include no name-calling, no swearing, no relative bashing, and so on. When a person feels violated emotionally, he or she will be quick to withdraw from future risk in developing intimacy. Brian and I came up with a "buzzing" rule to use during times of heated emotions. The other person could not talk during an argument until the first person had said all they

wanted and then made a "buzzing" sound kind of like on a game show. It was silly, but it worked. Sometimes the silliness of it contributed to making the mood a little lighter as well, and we ended up laughing about our "buzzes."

- *Creating a signal for stress.* Agree on a sign or clue that tells the other spouse when you have been hurt, disappointed, or angered. This can be as simple as lighting a candle, or putting a certain stuffed animal on your pillow. Then agree to discuss the topic in a public place that day or the next.
- *Lowering your expectations.* Actually, eliminate them! If you have no real expectations for your spouse, then whatever he or she does will be a bonus and a cause for a celebration.
- *Laughing.* Learn to laugh at your differences and even offenses. Rarely does one spouse deliberately set out to make the other one mad. Conflict often results from differences in gender, personalities, and expectations.[2]

Reclaiming intimacy, though, requires more than just learning how to deal with disappointment and differences. It requires proactively seeking it. The apostle Peter teaches how to handle disappointments in relationships. Following his writing on the duties of a wife and husband, Peter writes, "Let all be . . . not returning evil for evil, or insult for insult, but giving a blessing instead; for you were called for the very purpose that you might inherit a blessing" (1 Peter 3:8–9).

Not only are we to refrain from doing hurtful things when disappointed but, also, we are to repay the disappointment with a blessing. Peter continues, "And let him turn away from evil and do good; let him seek peace and pursue it" (v. 11). *We must pursue it.* Achieving marital intimacy, like achieving authentic intimacy with the Lord, is a quest. It is a challenge. It cannot be bought or bargained for. It is attained only by taking special care.

Shortly before we moved as missionaries to Kenya, Brian and I sat down to discuss how to get through the huge transition celebrating, and not stressed, on the other end. Brian's suggestion mirrored that of pursuing intimacy. "We have to, even when we are busy and tired, set aside time to talk and relate to each other personally several times every day—morning, noon, and night, at a minimum. We have to stay connected." I added that we have to stay consistently "intimately" connected as well. No arguments there.

Below are some suggestions that might assist in your quest for marital intimacy:

- Ask God daily to nurture romantic and giving love in your marriage.
- Eliminate as many negatives as possible. Avoid criticism. Employ positives. Offer compliments. Look for opportunities to build up your spouse.
- Arrange a series of enjoyable experiences based on emotional closeness alongside experiences based on physical closeness.
- Cultivate the right climate for your mate to experience freedom with you and desire for you. That will allow him or her to feel safe (or even to mess up).
- Frequently offer the physical stimulus of closeness, affection, touching, and eye contact without sexual arousal being the only goal.
- Use your God-given gift of imagination to encourage love in your own mind. Stop thinking about the hundreds of insignificant things that zap your energies, and focus instead on the one who would really benefit from your energy.

A few months after Brian graduated from seminary, he got a full-time job offer for a managerial position at the seminary. The job would include perks such as free tuition if he wanted to continue his education in the future.

When we had originally accepted the call to seminary as a "God-thing," we assumed that God would provide for His thing. As a result, we cut up our credit cards, and one of us stayed home with the children at all times, thus limiting work opportunities and, as a result, income. And God did wonderfully provide for us during the entire time. He met all of our needs and even left us with no student loans at graduation.

We had been the recipient of God's provision through various ways—a check in the mail here, a special job there. I admit, though, that my flesh had grown desirous of knowing exactly what we could count on financially and when. The full-time salary Brian was offered on graduation tempted me simply because it would have been predictable.

Brian, however, turned the job down.

My flesh felt like strangling him and calling into question his sanity, but my spirit set out to honor him. Brian told me that he did not believe God was leading him to take this position but wanted him to remain open for something else He was planning. So I got down on my knees beside him and prayed a prayer of thanksgiving. And yes, I meant it. My flesh may desire consistency in income, but my spirit has tasted how sweet it is to daily trust Jesus and how peaceful it is to rest in God-ordained roles.

A few months later, we received a request to come and minister to a group of people in East Africa. Going into the mission field had never been our intention while attending seminary. Yet the more we prayed and sought God's leading, the more it appeared that this request was the work of His hand. If moving to Texas to attend seminary had been a culture shock, I could only imagine what moving to East Africa would be like. I wanted to be extra certain that this was what God wanted.

We sought confirmation in a number of ways over the next few months and believed that this was the path God was asking us to walk. So we accepted. As part of our pre-field training, we were asked to attend a cross-cultural school in Bakersfield, California. So we packed up our things, rented out our home, and moved to Bakersfield.

It was August. Bakersfield greeted us warmly—very warmly. It's located in a desert. Did I mention it was August?

One couldn't tell, though, driving around the city, that Bakersfield is anywhere near a desert. Tall palm trees grow alongside pines and tremendous magnolias. The interstates are lined with bushes, flowers, and trees. Lawns are meticulously cared for in most parts of town. Groves of orange trees grow next to fields of grapes and other fruit. Bakersfield appears lush. That is, until you hit the edge of town. Then barren, empty desert stretches for miles. Even the tumbleweed doesn't tumble through that part of Bakersfield. The ground is scorching hot and dry.

The city of Bakersfield, though, is fertile and produces a huge percentage of the world's fruit and almonds because a river runs through it. The Kern River has been directed in irrigation channels down the mountains, through the valleys, and into Bakersfield. Water is everywhere here. And, as a result, so is life.

I love Bakersfield, because it's a reflection of life—a life resting in Jesus. No matter how much I like to convince myself otherwise, I am a sinner and totally depraved. Nothing good originates from within me. God tells us clearly that there is none righteous, not one—there is none who does good, and no one who seeks God.

My soul is a desert—it is dry, and it is barren. My marriage is a desert—it is helpless, and it is empty. My life is a desert—it is unsightly, and it is powerless. Yet Jesus flows from the highest mountain of heaven to bring His living water into my desert.

If ten years ago I'd been told that I would cherish my marriage as something sacred, I wouldn't have believed it. Tolerable maybe, but not sacred. That's because a desert looks hopeless. Yet when Jesus flooded our hearts with His love, He brought life to our marriage, causing our affections to blossom with the scent of His grace. He turned a desert into a lush and living delight.

Allow me to stress one point: The intimacy in my marriage was not reclaimed overnight. The blooming of a soul is often a lengthy process, especially when consequences from sin have seared the spirit. Yet intimacy did come and continues to come with each new drop of Jesus' life-giving water. Here are a few suggestions to help irrigate your intimacy:

- Ask God daily to reveal your personal weaknesses in fulfilling your role in your marriage. Ask God for the strength to grow in these areas.
- Ask God daily to reveal to your spouse his or her personal weaknesses in fulfilling his or her role as well as to grant the grace to grow in those areas.
- Attend a couple of different Christian marriage conferences. They're fun. The speakers are usually entertaining as well as edifying. It's a great excuse to spend some one-on-one time together.[3]
- Do a personal Bible study on your role in marriage. Look at all the Bible passages that deal with the way a wife or husband should handle things, and what the responsibilities of each role are.
- Check out some good Christian books written specifically on marriage and the roles within a marriage.
- And most importantly, get to know Jesus. Really get to know Him.

God has shown His grace to me. According to God's ancient laws, Brian and I would have been stoned to death for our sin of premarital sex. Yet in God's mercy, through the sacrifice of Christ, we have been forgiven and our guilt taken away. And through our repentance, through our looking to Jesus, He has created love in our life, blessing us with an intimacy for which I am eternally grateful.

Over a decade ago, in my quest for intimacy, I stepped off the path to authentic intimacy and found only a counterfeit intimacy. Like Alice's imaginary land beyond the looking glass, premarital sex was not the wonderland I had expected. And just as Alice was glad when she woke up from her dream, I'm glad to now be back in reality. I have seen the madness that can result from following selfish desires.

This chapter began with a list of things that people have learned over the course of their lives. Here are a couple of my own. A twenty-nine-year-old woman has learned the difference between the counterfeit intimacy that comes with putting one's hope in people and things, and the authentic intimacy that is found in wholeness with God. She has also learned that intimacy, cradled in the bosom of the Beloved, will grow and flourish.

Do I hear an Amen?

Epilogue

While recovering from the birth of our second daughter, I had the perfect excuse to sit back and watch the 1992 Olympic games in their entirety. My new baby and I bonded over track-and-field, baseball games, and gymnastics. We hung out together, savoring each moment. I loved Barcelona!

One afternoon proved more memorable than the others. Eight athletes stepped up to their starting blocks for the four-hundred-meter run. None were from America, and it was just a semifinal. So a nap on the couch with my baby girl seemed quite appealing. Yet when the starting gun cracked, I watched, cheering for no one in particular.

The runners shot out of the blocks and swooped around the curve. They raced down the backstretch and around the final turn. Arms pumped rhythmically. Dreams hung in the balance.

One runner suddenly pulled up in what appeared to be excruciating pain. He fell face first, his dreams melting with the tears on his cheeks. The runner's name was Derek Redmond.

Sports Illustrated recorded it this way:

As the medical attendants were approaching, Redmond
fought to his feet. "It was animal instinct," he would say
later. He set out hopping, in a crazed attempt to finish the
race. When he reached the stretch, a large man in a T-shirt
came out of the stands, hurled aside a security guard and
ran to Redmond, embracing him. This was Jim Redmond.
Derek's father.

"You don't have to do this," he told his weeping son.
"Yes, I do," said Derek. "Well, then," said Jim, "we're going to finish this together." And they did. Fighting off security men, the son's head sometimes buried in his father's
shoulder, they stayed in Derek's lane to the end, as the
crowd gaped, then rose, howled and wept.[1]

Chalk it up to postpartum blues, but a floodgate opened, and
my pillow was soaked. "Yay!" I shouted. (Sniff, sniff.) "Yay!"

Derek hadn't broken any record; nor would anyone be escort-
ing him to the podium. But in less than a minute, he had become
an international symbol. His claim to fame—he'd finished what
he'd begun. Receiving a standing ovation at the end of his race,
Derek heard thundering applause.

Few people can name the athlete who won the gold medal in
the men's four hundred that day. But the name Derek Redmond
and the image of him crossing the line, his head on his father's
shoulder, still melts hearts nearly a decade later.

That's because we all can identify with him. We all have fallen
in one way or another. We all have set out to reach a goal, only to
come up short because of our own failings. We all have found
ourselves face down, the heat of the track scorching our souls.

If you have engaged in premarital sex, you know what it's like to
see the finish line waver like a mirage in the distance. The marital
intimacy you had dreamed about may have suffered setbacks early

on in the race. But God is not as concerned with time as He is with distance. He is not concerned with how fast we finish, but that we finish well.

If your past has left you in a crumpled heap on the track, now is the time to get back up. Lean on your heavenly Father; bury your head in His shoulder. He has come down from His heavenly throne to help you. Tell Him you need to finish the race. He alone has the strength to help you cross the finish line.

Can you hear Him? "We're going to finish this race together."

I look forward to seeing you at the finish line.

Notes

Chapter 1: Losing My Way

1. "Should Condoms Be Distributed in Schools?" *Prioritie* 6 (1994).
2. *Prime Time Live,* NBC, 12 August 1998.
3. "TV's Frisky Family Values," *U.S. News & World Report,* 15 April 1996. A week's worth of prime-time entertainment on ABC, CBS, NBC, and Fox was monitored in mid-March 1996.
4. James Poniewozik, "Sex on TV Is Not . . . Not Sexy!" *Time,* 2 August 1999.
5. Jane Hall, "We're Listening, Ted," *Los Angeles Times,* Calendar Section, 3 April 1994.
6. "Cosmo Confessions," *Cosmopolitan,* October 1999.
7. "Glamour's Super Sex Challenge," *Glamour,* July 1999.
8. Lisa Sussman, "Twelve Cool Ways to Make Your Love Last," *YM: Young and Modern,* August 1998.
9. Dennis Rainey, *Preparing for Marriage* (California: Gospel Light, 1997).
10. Josh McDowell and Dick Day, *Why Wait?* (Nashville: Nelson, 1987).

11. Evelyn Millis Duvall, *Facts of Love and Life for Teen-Agers* (New York: Association Press, 1950).

12. Ibid.

13. Brent Curtis and John Eldredge, *The Sacred Romance* (Nashville: Nelson, 1997).

14. Willard Harley, interview by the author, Dallas, Texas, 15 July 1998.

15. Oswald Chambers, *My Utmost for His Highest* (Grand Rapids: Discovery House, 1992).

Chapter 2: My True Longing

1. Larry Crabb, *Inside Out* (Colorado Springs: NavPress, 1988).

2. James Strong, *The New Strong's Exhaustive Concordance of the Bible* (Nashville: Nelson, 1995).

3. Kenneth L. Barker and John R. Kohlenberger III, eds., *NIV Bible Commentary,* vol. 2, *New Testament* (Grand Rapids: Zondervan, 1994).

4. C. S. Lewis, *Mere Christianity,* rev. ed. (New York: Touchstone, 1996).

5. Interview with Bob Bartlett, "Intimacy 101 for Teens," *U.S. Catholic,* August 1999.

6. Sandra Anderson, *Angels Can Fall* (Enumclaw, Wash.: WinePress, 1998).

7. Larry Crabb, *Inside Out* (Colorado Springs: NavPress, 1988).

8. Tony Evans, "Fasting for Your Mate," sermon given at Oak Cliff Bible Fellowship, 7 February 1999.

Chapter 3: Wounds of Love

1. Piaget's Stages of Cognitive Development.

Chapter 4: First Comes Love. Then Comes Baby. Then Comes Marriage in a Baby Carriage

1. "Revisiting 'The Baby Trap,'" *People*, 11 October 1999.
2. Everett L. Worthington Jr., *Counseling for Unplanned Pregnancy and Infertility* (Waco: Word, 1987).
3. John Stossel, *TEENS*, ABC, 5 September 1999.

Chapter 5: Not as Strong as We Think

1. Willard Harley, interview by the author, Dallas, Texas, 15 July 1998.
2. Tori Smart and Sandy Fertman, "I Had a Sexually Transmitted Disease," *Teen Magazine*, November 1997.
3. Deborah L. Shelton, "STD Numbers Higher Than Estimated," *American Medical News*, 28 December 1998.
4. Anonymous, *Aim for Success*, www.aim-for-success.org; INTERNET.
5. *Merriam Webster's Collegiate Dictionary*, 10th ed., s.v. "idol."
6. Dawson McAllister, *Focus on the Family Radio*, 4 February 1999.
7. *Merriam Webster's Collegiate Dictionary*, 10th ed., s.v. "intimate."
8. Tommy Nelson, "Intimacy," Song of Solomon Tape Series, Denton Bible Church, Texas.
9. Tony Evans, *The Urban Alternative*, May 1999.
10. Roger Hillerstrom, telephone interview with author, 10 February 1999.

Chapter 6: Despoiling the Temple

1. Francois Fenelon, *The Royal Way to the Cross* (Cape Cod, Mass.: Paraclete, 1982).

2. Gary Thomas, interview by the author, Dallas, Texas, November 1998.

3. I first heard this teaching idea as having originated from Dr. Ronald Allen, professor, Dallas Theological Seminary, Dallas, Texas.

Chapter 7: I Repent

1. Andrew Murray, *Confession and Forgiveness* (Grand Rapids: Zondervan, 1978).

2. Tony Evans, *The Urban Alternative*, 16 July 1999.

3. *Merriam Webster's Collegiate Dictionary,* 10th ed., s.v. "remorse."

4. Craig S. Keener, *The IVP Bible Background Commentary,* vol. 2, *New Testament* (Downers Grove, Ill.: InterVarsity, 1993).

5. Lewis Sperry Chafer, *Systematic Theology,* vol. 3 (Grand Rapids: Kregel, 1993).

6. Rich Mullins, "Hard to Get," *The Jesus Record,* Word Entertainment, 1998.

7. Interview with Bob Bartlett, "Intimacy 101 for Teens," *U.S. Catholic,* August 1999.

8. Jim Logan, *Reclaiming Surrendered Ground* (Chicago: Moody, 1995).

9. John Roger and Peter McWilliams, *Life 101* (Los Angeles: Prelude, 1991).

10. Dave Noel, "I Repent," *The Faithful,* Steve Green, Jillybird Music, 1998.

Chapter 8: Trust and Obey

1. *Chips* was a 1970s motorcycle cop television show.

2. Francois Fenelon, *Letting Go* (Springdale, Pa.: Whitaker House, 1973).

3. J. I. Packer, *Knowing God* (Downers Grove, Ill.: InterVarsity, 1973).

Chapter 9: I Want to Fall in Love with You

1. Gary Thomas, *Sacred Marriage* (Grand Rapids: Zondervan, 2000).

2. Larry Crabb, *Men and Women* (Grand Rapids: Zondervan, 1993).

3. Andrew Murray, *Humility* (Ft. Washington, Pa.: Christian Literature Crusade, 1995).

4. Mike Mason, *The Mystery of Marriage* (Portland, Ore.: Multnomah, 1985).

5. Tony Evans, sermon, Oak Cliff Bible Fellowship, 1999.

6. Two recommendations include: Gary Thomas, *The Glorious Pursuit: Embracing the Virtues of Christ* (Colorado Springs: NavPress, 1998); or Max Lucado, *Just Like Jesus* (Nashville: Nelson/Word, 1998).

7. Beth Moore, *Praying God's Word* (Nashville: Broadman and Holman, 2000).

8. C. S. Lewis, *Mere Christianity* (New York: Touchstone, 1996).

Chapter 10: Finding My Way

1. Mike Mason, *The Mystery of Marriage* (Portland, Ore.: Multnomah, 1985).

2. Two recommendations include: Tim LaHaye, *Opposites Attract: Bringing Out the Best in Your Spouse* (Eugene, Ore.: Harvest House, 1991); or Cynthia Ulrich Tobias, *The Way*

They Learn (Colorado Springs: Focus on the Family, 1994). (Although intended to be used as a parenting resource, the information in *The Way They Learn* can be applied to all ages.)

3. Two recommendations include: Family Life Marriage Conferences, 1-800-FL-TODAY, familylife.com, P.O. Box 23840, Little Rock, AR, 72221; or Walk Thru the Bible Marriage Conference, 1-800-868-9300, walkthru.org, 4201 N. Peachtree Road, Atlanta, GA, 30341.

Epilogue

1. Kenny Moore, "Ode to Joy," *Sports Illustrated,* 17 August 1992.